Living W

& Dying Well

A Sacramental View of Life and Death

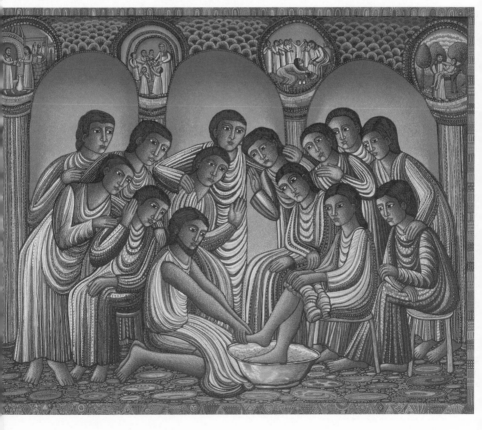

Living Well
& Dying Well

A Sacramental View of Life and Death

MARY ELLEN O'BRIEN

SHEED & WARD

Franklin, Wisconsin
Chicago

As an apostolate of the Priests of the Sacred Heart, a Catholic religious congregation, the mission of Sheed & Ward is to publish books of contemporary impact and enduring merit in Catholic Christian thought and action. The books published, however, reflect the opinion of their authors and are not meant to represent the official position of the Priests of the Sacred Heart.

2001

Sheed & Ward
7373 South Lovers Lane Road
Franklin, Wisconsin 53132
1-800-266-5564

Printed in the United States of America

Cover and interior design: Robin Booth

Cover art used: Washing of the Feet © 2000 by John August Swanson; Serigraph 21" by 26"; www.JohnAugustSwanson.com Used with permission.

Library of Congress Cataloging-in-Publication Data

O'Brien, MaryEllen.
    Living well & dying well : a sacramental view of life and death / MaryEllen O'Brien.
        p. cm.
    ISBN 1-58051-108-2
    1. Christian life—Catholic authors. I. Title: Living well and dying well. II. Title.

BX2350.3 .O27 2001
248.4'82—dc21

                                                                                                2001036511

1 2 3 4 5 / 04 03 02 01

Contents

IV

V

VI

VII

Acknowledgments

"We do not go it alone." This is the chief lesson of the art of living well and dying well found in the *Ars Vivendi* and *Ars Moriendi* tradition. And so a book reclaiming a wise and powerful tradition from an earlier time in the Church is also not born or written in solitary study, but comes to be through conversations and encouragement and the support of others—teachers living and dead, communities of faith, and the interest of all those who asked "What is your book about?" and responded with fascination and affirmation of the need for this kind of book in our time. I am grateful for their comments and for all the support of friends and colleagues.

This book began as my master's thesis at Catholic Theological Union in Chicago, when it was entitled *The* Ars Moriendi *Tradition: A Hermeneutic of the Art of Holy Dying in History and Contemporary Practice*. I first discovered and was captured by the beauty of the tradition in a seminar on sacramental theology that concentrated on death rituals. It became the focus of my study and later my thesis topic. I am deeply grateful for the interest this work generated with my publisher, Sheed & Ward, and co-publisher, Jeremy Langford, who saw its wisdom and value for a contemporary audience. I am also thankful for those teachers and readers who were part of my thesis work, and to those who read the manuscript, especially Father John Linnan, CSV, and Sister Dianne Bergant, CSA, of Catholic Theological Union.

The artists who have supported this work deserve my deep appreciation as well. Catya Plate of New York City generously shared her art and inspiration on the contemporary place of the *Ars Moriendi* in my earlier work and continues to contribute her ongoing support. And for the book's artistic beauty, I thank artist John August Swanson of Los Angeles for his immediate enthusiasm and generosity in being a part of this project with his glorious religious art and especially for the interpretation of *The Washing of the Feet* used on the cover. The "foot washing" connects us to living well as servants and disciples of Christ but also connects us directly to Christ's passion, which forms the heart of the meditations on the Art of Holy Living and Dying. The washing of the feet, after all, begins our annual "Great Liturgy," the Easter Triduum, and its roller-coaster ride into Holy Week and into the love, the passion, and the resurrection of Jesus—and all that his disciples endured with him along that road of faith.

Additionally, for the overall visual beauty of the book I thank Robin Booth, both for her friendship and encouragement throughout the project and for my good fortune at having her professional expertise as my designer.

I am grateful for my son, Leif, and his cheerful enthusiasm for my writing. Upon completion of the manuscript he gave me the thumbs-up sign and a hearty, "Cool, Mom!" He's pretty cool himself, at age nineteen.

And, finally, my deepest gratitude is extended to my teacher, Richard Fragomeni, who introduced me to the *Ars Moriendi* with his own giddy passion for such things, who directed my master's thesis, and who has guided me as spiritual mentor and teacher among teachers. He is a man whose brilliance is outdone only by his compassion. I am graced to have had his presence in my life, for he embodies the Art of Holy Living and embraces the Art of Holy Dying.

Artist's Notes

Washing of the Feet
JOHN AUGUST SWANSON © 2000
Serigraph
21" x 26"

I began working with the image of the washing of feet in 1989 with a mixed media painting. In 1999 I did a series of three acrylic paintings on the theme. The first of the three is the one that has been developed into this serigraph limited edition.

Fourteen large figures dominate the picture. A miniature scene is at the top of each of the four columns: Jesus and the woman at the well; the gift of wisdom to children, not to the worldly wise; Mary Magdalene washing the feet of Jesus; and the story of the Good Samaritan.

The theme of this picture encourages us to show love for all and true humility of spirit. I feel this ritual of the paschal event transcends particular religious observances and gives us a beautiful guide for our own lives. We are called to treat all with respect and serve in our community in different capacities.

—JOHN AUGUST SWANSON

Los Angeles artist *John August Swanson* is noted for his finely detailed and brilliantly colored paintings and original prints. His works are found in the Smithsonian Institution's National Museum of American History, London's Tate Gallery, the Vatican Museum's Collection of Modern Religious Art, and the Bibliothèque

Nationale in Paris. John August Swanson's paintings and limited-edition serigraphs are available from the Bergsma Gallery, Grand Rapids, Michigan (616-458-1776); full-color posters and cards of Mr. Swanson's work are available from the National Association for Hispanic Elderly. Proceeds benefit the association's programs of employment and housing for low-income seniors. For information, contact: National Association of Hispanic Elderly, 234 East Colorado Blvd., Suite 300, Pasadena, CA 91101 (626-564-1988). Website: http://www.JohnAugustSwanson.com

About the Cover

Author's Notes

I was introduced to the work of John August Swanson when I first arrived in Chicago to attend graduate school. In the hallways and rooms of Catholic Theological Union, where icons and artistry accompany the buzz of teaching and learning, there appeared, here and there, the distinctive, wildly colorful spiritual art of Mr. Swanson. Later, I began to see more of his art at my own Chicago church, where every feast and season seemed an occasion for an easel to be set up and his works displayed.

The artist is instantly recognizable in his work, and his art always evoked deep pleasure and equally deep reflection within me whenever my eyes locked onto one of his paintings. The depth of biblical stories reach out, the great emotion of saints and sinners of both testaments is palpable, and the remarkable gift of God given to Mr. Swanson for the benefit of the Body of Christ is alive for all to see. So it should come as no surprise that when it came time to consider a cover for my first book, John August Swanson's art was my first choice.

I contacted Mr. Swanson and told him about the book. To my great joy, he agreed to see if we could find just the right piece of art from his body of work. The tradition of the *Ars Moriendi*, after all, was as much a visual tradition as a literary one in its medieval and Renaissance heyday.

After much discussion and after considering quite a few paintings, I was sure he did indeed have a painting that met my expectations: *The Washing of the Feet* said it all.

In *The Washing of the Feet*, we see the Art of Holy Living demonstrated in the teachings of the Master, Jesus. With Jesus and the disciples engaged in this extraordinary act of service and humility, where even the Master washes the feet of the disciples, we witness the summation of *Living Well*: the community of faith gathered together; acts of service; humility, the remedy to the spiritual crisis of pride; prayer and love abounding. And all of this occurs with the specter of Jesus' crucifixion close at hand. Temptations also abound. We know this because we know what comes next: Judas' betrayal; Peter's denial; the crisis of despair, guilt, and doubt; and the temptation to the loss of faith all loom in the background of the gospel story of the washing of the feet.

When I looked at Mr. Swanson's painting, I knew we had the perfect cover. For a book that recalls the tradition of holy dying for today must also recall holy living, the necessary forerunner. A book that calls for community, service, and deep care for one another in the process of loss, dying, and grief is a book that calls for us to wash one another's feet, with all the rich symbolism that the biblical image implies. And a book that calls for a reclamation of the rich *Ars Vivendi* and *Ars Moriendi* tradition (Holy Living and Holy Dying) also speaks with the specter of our human vulnerability close at hand. We too will die. Jesus showed us how to approach death, after he first taught us how to live. Notice as you read, that some of the most prominent saints that are called upon in the traditional prayers are also portrayed in *The Washing of the Feet*: Mary, Mary Magdalene, Saint Peter, and the other apostles—all were integral to the imagination and prayers of our forebearers for holy lives and a holy death. So it is with great joy that the cover art is from such an artistic master himself, John August Swanson, and that it so vividly portrays the spirituality described in this book.

From Little Italy in Chicago where I live and pray, Grazie.

Introduction

The Art of Living Well and Dying Well

Fifteenth-century Western Europe was chaotic: wars, rampant disease, high infant mortality, short life spans, pervasive illiteracy. Haves and have-nots competed for limited resources, theatrical spectacles indulged in an intense morbidity, and the Black Plague dominated daily life. Yet, it was against this impoverished and vulnerable backdrop that wonderfully wise, simple, and compassionate spiritual guides for "dying well" emerged. The tradition was known by its Latin name, the *Ars Bene Moriendi*, or simply *Ars Moriendi*, which translates to "The Art of Dying Well," or "The Art of Holy Dying." The continent was steeped in death as Europeans tried to manage an out-of-control plague, engaged in wars and other violent outbreaks, and faced the reality of an average life expectancy of only forty years. Everyone was familiar with the face of death. So familiar that the populace created the danse macabre for their theaters and were given to intense displays of emotion, if and when they paid attention to spiritual matters at all. Theater was a medium to literally act out what scholar Nancy Lee Beaty called the "necromania" of their time.[1] The elaborate staging of the danse macabre, with a costumed cadaver, "Le Mort," leading a hapless parade of mortals of all social ranks, from peasant to prince, pope to monk, and maiden to queen, into the captivity of death was met with roars of approval from medieval audiences. "Le Mort" would be portrayed in various stages of decomposition, leading the end-of-life procession like a demented pied piper—to the delight of theatergoers! At least on stage, death was under the control of a director and the actors. The danse macabre provided the citizenry a dramatic release for the fears and anxieties about the world they lived in and allowed them to mock death and laugh at its expense, while knowing that their own lives were as fleeting and fragile as "bubbles." The bubble was the image Jeremy Taylor, the Anglican writer of *Holy Dying*, would use to teach his flock about living well and dying well. Taylor claimed the image from a Greek proverb and elaborated on it extensively for his seventeenth-century readers.

These times were marked by disinterest in faith and spirituality until death demanded spiritual attention. Survival took enough of a toll on the minds and souls of the people in daily life. Religion was not a high priority when securing food, shelter, and defenses sapped the energy for all but the elite and educated classes. Life was very hard and very, very short. What the handbooks on dying well did, then, was to help form the consciences of people who had little or no religious instruction. In this way, individuals followed the handbook, assisted one another, and prepared one another and themselves for their own deaths. Thus, they learned to pray and be deeply concerned about their fellow human beings.

Like these late medieval Europeans, we also put death on stage. We have our own "Le Morts" in horror and action movies. We, too, like to mock death. We also turn to gallows humor when faced with incomprehensible violence or disease and find ways to cope by acting out our fears. Books and films—filled with fright and fantasy, horror and death—may serve the same purpose as the danse macabre once did. Stephen King has suggested as much in his role as literary prince of the macabre for our own time.

In the late fourteenth century, when the handbooks for dying well first appeared, the untamed emotions of popular culture bordered on religious apathy. Sure, the dying person wanted a priest present at death, but most people kept religion at a safe distance until they themselves invited it in. Both the Dominicans and the Franciscans attempted to combat this religious indifference and deathbed conversion mentality. Yet these two religious orders, which dominated Western Europe's religious teaching in late medieval times, chose two very different approaches to rattle the bones of the faithless and the endangered souls they encountered.

The Dominicans chose fierce preaching with a sharp edge of damnation in hopes of frightening the indifferent masses back to the arms of Mother Church. The Franciscans, on the other hand, hoped to overcome indifference by preaching love, especially love as demonstrated by Christ on the cross. The Franciscans turned over and over again to the Passion of Christ as the model for both love and for living well and dying well. In turn, the Passion of Christ and the influence of the Franciscans dominated these handbooks.

Historians and scholars have accused both orders of extremism, whether their methods were emotional or intellectual. According to Beatty, "skulls, worms, fire, and brimstone were, in one way or another, singularly useful weapons in the battle for God and the Church."[2]

With literacy levels low and emotional responses to drama, love, and hellfire preaching high, the fifteenth century was a melodramatic theatrical setting in its own right. The masses of people were not sensitive to spiritual subtleties and nuances. The authorities often treated them like children who needed blunt and dramatic messages, such as the danse macabre or the preaching methods of the traveling disciples of Saint Dominic and Saint Francis, to shake their indifference wide open.

Later in the course of the history of the *Ars Moriendi*, this bluntness would change. Jeremy Taylor would write highly sophisticated treatises on living well and dying well, filled, as they were, with classical references and highly developed rhetoric for an equally well-educated reader. In this way, the genre of the *Ars Moriendi* evolved over a three-hundred-year period. From picture books for the illiterate, coupled with high-intensity preaching, to sophisticated and, one could say, elitist renderings, the genre flourished. It even bridged the Protestant Reformation, being a tradition that both Roman Catholics and the reformers could embrace, albeit with differing emphases. The Catholic books stressed sacramental life, especially liturgy and prayer and community, while the reformers emphasized a more individualistic and personal approach to behavior and living a moral life. From the first anonymous tracts by William Caxton's press in 1490 to the height of Jeremy Taylor's literary excellence in the seventeenth century to the waning years of the genre as the eighteenth century loomed, the *Ars Moriendi* handbooks provided spiritual guidance and liturgical rituals for the women and men of Christian Europe.

In this present reclamation of the art of holy living and holy dying for our own time, there are riches to be mined that can be dusted off and made to glimmer in the darkness of loss and death, so that we too may live well and die a peaceful death in faith and hope with Christ, in whom we place all hope. We can shake off the melodrama and keep the glimmering treasures. For five hundred years later, things are not so different. We have our own plagues around the globe, wars continue to erupt and throw nations into chaos, and international terrorism puts before us a new kind of evil. We still see the haves and the have-nots, as entire countries are labeled with the tag *Third World* to denote their primitive technology, political upheaval, and economic instability. Even the "have" nations confront new forms of chaos as First World countries such as the United States face never-before-seen violence in which children turn guns on other children, workers on fellow workers, and rage and death spill onto our streets.

When you think about it further, life is not so different for us as it was for our fifteenth-century predecessors. True, we live longer, but we have new problems confronting our aging population. We see infants live to become healthy young children, but we inhabit a world with an overwhelmingly high rate of abortion, child poverty, abuse, neglect, illness, and death. We have access to unprecedented resources and technologies, but the gap between the haves and the have-nots continues to widen.

What separates us from our predecessors, however, is that we lack the courage, community, and comfort with which they faced life and death. While we hide from and avoid death wherever possible, they not only lived with it everyday but they also developed a "way of dying" so profound that, if we listen, it continues to speak to us today. Maybe just a touch of their "emotionality" would do us some good, to awaken us to our own mortality and to our spiritual responsibilities to one another.

In the face of chaos, our predecessors banded together, attended liturgies, watched out for one another, and prayed as a community. And they wrote down or depicted in art what they observed in the process of dying. Out of their experience and hard-earned wisdom came *The Art of Holy Dying*–handbooks for learning the art of dying well. Eventually blockbooks, or picture books, were made for the illiterate so that everyone could learn this necessary art on the road to better living and peaceful dying.

At first these visual depictions and textual guides for dying well appeared anonymously and could be found everywhere. The blockbooks, as they were called, were made from a series of eleven woodcuts common across Europe. They depicted five great temptations and five spiritual remedies that one could anticipate in the final journey toward death. The eleventh woodcut represented death and the departure of the soul safely into the Kingdom of God, carried away by angels.

As the plague receded and the tradition matured, it was obvious there was more to dying well than perfecting the deathbed scene. No one can die well and peacefully, it was decided, if they have not lived well. Living well then became the first priority. Spiritual leaders such as

Jeremy Taylor relied on classical references, but Taylor was also the first to rely heavily on Scripture, writing with the assumption that his readers were familiar with both the Bible and the ancient philosophers. Taylor's premier book was called:

> *The Rule and Exercises of Holy Dying: in which are described The Means and Instruments of preparing our selves, and others respectively, for a Blessed Death: and the remedies against the evils and temptations proper to the state of Siknesse. Together with Prayers and Acts of Vertue to be used by sick and dying persons, or by others standing in their attendance. To which are added, Rules for the Visitation of the Sick, and offices proper for that ministry.*

Whew! That's quite a subtitle, and it is a long way from the earliest published text in the genre, *The Arte & Crafte to Know Well to Dye*, which was a translation of an anonymous French text published by William Caxton in 1490 England.

In between Caxton and Taylor, many different texts existed that all held in common a core structure. For the Roman Catholic versions, this structure was sixfold: 1) the commendation of death; 2) the five temptations and remedies; 3) the interrogations, or scrutinies of the dying person, to be conducted by a priest, if at all possible; 4) rules of conduct in dying and prayers for individual use modeled on the Passion of Christ; 5) responsibilities of deathbed assistants for the dying person and for their own spiritual welfare; and 6) prayers of passage from this world to the next to be prayed with the dying person.

Reception of the final sacrament of penance and Eucharist were extremely important to the people who hoped to die well and be accompanied by angels, saints, and the Virgin Mary.

In recent years there has been a renewed interest in the *Ars Moriendi* tradition. Yale University's School of Medicine even held a conference on the subject in 1994. The interest emerges from a desire to counter a cultural denial of death, whereby people hide from its inevitability and try to sanitize its very existence. The hospice movement has also made an important impact on the way we view and deal with death in the United States. Health care professionals, pastoral ministers, clergy, philosophers, and scholars alike have begun to see the wisdom of the art of dying well. What has been striking, however, is that the tradition is generally being reclaimed from outside its religious and spiritual heritage. Dying well has become a philosophy and perhaps even a euphemism for assisted suicide. Moreover, practical suggestions are extracted from the tradition so we get the wisdom without the religious commitment or context.

My purpose in writing this book is to reclaim the wholeness of the *Ars Moriendi* tradition as a religious and deeply spiritual practice that has much to teach us. It is, in fact, both a spirituality of death and dying as well as living fully. Roman Catholic in its origin and early development, the *Ars Moriendi* became an early example of ecumenism in its transition across the Reformation, embraced by both Catholics and reformers. It continues to speak to Christians today.

The core of the tradition—the five spiritual temptations and remedies—are still valid today. For the purposes of this volume, I call the temptations "spiritual crises," thus using more contemporary language without losing the depth of the experience. These are truly individual crises that need to be identified, named, and embraced. The remedies not only remain valid but they also present a serious challenge to our culture because they call us to prayer and communal support. The kind of intimate care and support suggested by this volume is so sorely lacking in our culture that a retrieval of it truly will take commitment and an extension of ourselves in our day-to-day lives. In our churches as well the call to reclaim community must be more than just Sunday liturgy and hospitality sessions afterward. Community means getting involved with one another, praying communally in liturgies and, more intimately, being there for one another, as we face everyday struggles, the inevitability of death, and the crises associated with it. In walking alongside one another in this journey, we not only become generous people but we also prepare ourselves for our own death. We *practice the art of holy living and dying.*

In this simple introductory volume to a spiritual discipline that flourished for three hundred years, I will sketch out the core principles and provide meditations and prayers for both personal and communal use. All of the meditations are original and may be prayed as a multi-voice piece, within a liturgy, or simply used for solo reading and meditation. The prayers included here are a mix of ancient sources and my original work. I liken this book to a pilgrimage. We will travel through the corridors of dying and meet the cast of characters whose wisdom helps us on our way through life and death. Some of these characters are mythical, some historical, some reflect various religious imaginations from history and cultures other than North American, and some reflect our own time and place. All of them teach us what it means to live well and die well.

This pilgrimage also borrows from the ancient concept of stational liturgies, movable liturgies that took place in different locations as the bishop or teacher traveled a particular region, with the pilgrims going to each site. Over time the beautiful tradition begun by the Franciscan friars called the Way of the Cross has developed into what we today refer to as the stations of the cross, whereby we move from station to station in our liturgy of prayer and meditation on the Passion of Christ. Likewise, the *Ars Moriendi* is a kind of pilgrimage in which we move through stations on the journey of life through death to the afterlife.

Another type of stational liturgy and pilgrimage is our sacramental life as Catholic Christians. Cradle to grave, we journey in a sacramental cycle of life and death. We enter our life of faith through baptism. If we are baptized as infants or children, we embark on the faith journey at the very beginning of our lives, sustained and taught in the faith by parents, sponsors, other relatives, and a community of faith. If we are baptized as adults, we are reborn in faith, daughters and sons of God, also supported by sponsors and a community of faith. In baptism we symbolically die in order to rise with Christ in new life. From the outset, our sacramental life introduces us to death. We die in order to live. The life we are born into is submerged in baptismal waters, in order for us to rise out of the water and live with the risen Christ in newness of life and spirit. We are empowered by our baptism to live in faith, and we are charged with the responsibility of supporting others in the faith by virtue of our baptism. We are encouraged with baptismal vows to live as Christians, remembering always who we are in Christ. So the door to the principles of *living well* opens for us, through water and through the Spirit. In the name of the Father and of the Son and of the Holy Spirit, we are introduced to life by faith, life according to the Gospel of Christ. In the name of the Trinity, we symbolically die with Christ to begin the journey of living well. Having such a gracious start to our lives in sacramental grace, we are invited to face our eventual deaths in the peace of Christ.

At stations along the way, we stop and sacramentalize our lives anew, with sacraments of further initiation, sacraments of healing, and sacraments of commitment. Stations of life, these sacraments are moments of great spiritual importance, even if we don't always fully understand them at the time. We prepare for our first Eucharist with great care, whether as children or as adults in the Rite of Christian Initiation for Adults (R.C.I.A.) program. Thus we are initiated into our lifelong practice of spiritual care, nourishment, and liturgical worship through the regular reception of the body and blood of Christ—Holy Communion. We learn that the Eucharist is a weekly practice for our spiritual benefit, and for the benefit of the whole community. This is a station, a pause in the rhythm of life, that we are invited to visit regularly. Through participation in the eucharistic liturgy we form the good spiritual habit of celebrating the Eucharist with others in the Body of Christ, the Church, and, in particular, our local worship communities. Through baptism and the Eucharist, the stage is set for living well, with the foundations laid out before us.

To further strengthen us, the sacrament of confirmation is conferred upon us at a time deemed appropriate for young Catholics (which may vary in different dioceses), or as part of the rites of initiation for adults. After confirmation, the Catholic Christian is considered fully initiated, responsible enough to live and share the faith, enabled by the power of the Holy Spirit.

Along the sacramental way we also learn about sacraments of healing, such as penance and reconciliation and the anointing of the sick. The sacrament of penance and reconciliation is spiritual medicine for our souls, where confession of sin, the narrative of our lives, keeps us cleansed and free, and where the prayer of the Church and the amendments we make to our lives help us to stay the course of living well. We have in this wonderful sacrament a sacred place to bring our failings, our faults, and our brokenness, and to seek the healing power of truth, accountability, and forgiveness. This sacrament also becomes part of our final journey in death, part of the reception of final sacraments. When the sacrament of penance and reconciliation has become a cherished part of our spiritual lives, it will easily flow into our final days as well. Our secrets by then will be few, if we have lived well and cared well for our souls. We will then more easily embrace a final confession and more readily believe that we are forgiven and blessed by God. The sacramental life offers us practices for living well, and when embraced, these practices form our consciences in such a way as to alleviate the crises that we will face in life's losses, especially in our inevitable rendezvous with death.

The anointing of the sick is, according to the official rites of the Roman Catholic Church, "the proper sacrament for those Christians whose health is seriously impaired by sickness or old age."[3] Our predecessors received what was formerly known as *extreme unction*, the last rites, including the anointing of the sick. And in some cases, they recovered from the serious illness, compelled to live better lives having been spared death. Today the sacrament of the sick is available to those who are seriously ill, or facing major surgery, as well as to those who are confronting imminent death. When we receive the gift of the sacrament of the anointing of the sick, we are embracing ourselves, body and soul, as sacramental human beings, worthy of the highest level of spiritual care, and responsible to live out our baptismal vows in all circumstances. We are acknowledging that our illnesses cannot take away our God-given dignity. Even our illnesses are sacred. So we are anointed, we are prayed for, and, if possible, we receive Communion.

In the final sacraments, our Eucharist is referred to as *Viaticum*. The word *Viaticum* means "food for the journey." What a lovely image for the dying person! "Take and eat," for the journey into the next world. The Church tells us, "The celebration of Eucharist as Viaticum, food for the passage through death to eternal life, is the sacrament proper to the dying Christian. It is the completion and crown of the Christian life on earth, signifying that the Christian follows the Lord to eternal glory and the banquet of the heavenly kingdom."[4] See how, even in death, the language of a journey, of pilgrimage, or passage, remains with us? We move to the next station, life eternally with Christ, prepared by sacraments just as we were brought into our faith by sacrament.

For many Christian pilgrims in adult life, there will also be a sacrament of commitment: holy matrimony and holy orders are the two sacraments of life commitment. When making a life commitment of the magnitude of marriage or ordination to the priesthood, Catholic Christians again turn to sacrament, making these commitments public, supported by the community of faith, and woven into other sacraments of accompaniment as well. Taking the sacrament of penance and reconciliation is advisable before accepting these life commitments. Most often, marriage is celebrated within a eucharistic liturgy (though not required). Holy orders always is. Both life commitments are publicly blessed, held up as extraordinarily sacred, and entwined with the rich symbolism of sacramental celebration.

So we begin our contemporary pilgrimage through the tradition of living well and dying well by actively remembering the living tradition of Scripture, church teaching, the sacraments, and the stations of the cross. Each station in this book includes a reproduction of the fifteenth-century German woodcuts that formed the "xylographic," or picture book editions of the *Ars Moriendi* handbooks. At each station we will address a spiritual crisis, explore the spiritual remedy, and attempt to link it to our own time and lives. Then we will engage in a guided meditation that may be used either with a group or individually. Last, at each station we will pray before moving on to the next stop on our pilgrimage.

This, then, is the itinerary for our pilgrimage. Chapters one through five take us through the spiritual crises and remedies. Chapter six reflects the end of the crises as death takes place. Chapter seven is a side trip to an older, yet similar tradition among the Celtic Christians of Ireland. And the conclusion brings our pilgrimage to a close and routes us back home. The chapters dealing with spiritual crises and remedies include a Scripture selection to meditate upon, reflections from the tradition, a meditation, and a closing prayer. As with all pilgrimages, we hope to return from the experience changed in a positive way. Pilgrimage is synonymous with change—it is the intention upon embarking on the journey and the goal upon return: to grow and change according to God's will in our lives. May Christ, our light and salvation, be present for us throughout the stations and every moment of our lives. Let us begin.

Dedication

• • •

To the young women of the Class of 2003,
McAuley Liberal Arts High School
Chicago
"Live well, and the peace of Christ be with you always."

· 1 ·

The First
Spiritual Crisis
and Remedy

LOSS OF FAITH

IN THIS FIRST WOODCUT we meet Moriens, the medieval Everyman, who is pictured on his deathbed. He is depicted as being about forty, which was the average lifespan during that time. Devils surround the bed. One devil holds a scroll, accusing Moriens of all manner of evil. Another devil points to an idolatrous king and queen, inferring that Moriens is guilty of idolatry. Still another devil points to a man about to cut his own throat. This is especially noteworthy, as the loss of faith could lead to suicide in one overcome by the crisis, or "temptation," as it was known then. There is also the figure of a woman wearing only a loincloth and carrying rods and a scourge. And finally there is the devil that prevents Moriens from seeing God the Father, Jesus Christ, and the Virgin Mary, even though they are very much present.[1] There is great significance in this diabolical attempt to convince Moriens that he is alone, save for the devils that torment him. Moriens needs help!

Crisis:
Loss of Faith

Now faith is the assurance of things hoped for,
the conviction of things not seen.
HEBREWS 11:1

. . .

The spiritual mentors who birthed the Catholic tradition of the *Ars Moriendi* established one essential truth at the outset: *Faith* is the foundation of all health. *All health.* What they were saying centuries ago is very much like the rediscovery of the mind-body connection in health care today. Faith is like breath, in other words. We cannot live without breath, it is the essence of life, even though it is invisible. We also cannot live in good health without faith, which is every bit as essential, and is also not always easy to see. As the evidence of breath is apparent in our living and moving and the beating of our hearts, so too is the evidence of faith apparent in our living *well*, moving in grace and peace, and having hearts filled with love. Just as we must breathe, we must have faith in order to live well. That is the cornerstone of the *Ars Vivendi* and the *Ars Moriendi*: The art of living well and the art of dying well. Faith comes by hearing, and hearing by the word of God, we are told in Saint Paul's Epistle to the Romans. So we encourage one another with words of faith, songs of faith, and stories of faith, old and new.

Faith is a gift, available to those who seek it. It's a gift we need, as much as we need the gifts of food, shelter, and clothing in order to live. Faith is a guiding source of courage, of wisdom, and of peace, without which we falter in dark nights of the soul.

The Hebrew word frequently used to denote the Spirit of God in Scripture is the same as the word for breath—*ruah*. Breath was seen as the perfect metaphor for Spirit, as it gives life.

Those who developed the art of living well and dying well knew that if faith faltered the whole body would suffer. If our breath becomes labored and heavy, our entire system weakens. If we stop breathing, we die. So it is with faith. If faith is truly endangered or terribly compromised, the whole life of the person is in danger. The mind, body, and spirit connection is real. If one's faith is healthy, everything else is healthy. But unlike our bodies, which will someday fail us, our faith will carry us through the transformation of life into eternal life with Christ.

Our predecessors approached life holistically. Their wisdom led to deeper living and a peaceful ending to life. They knew that through spiritual practices and careful presence to one another in life and in death, healing is made possible in spirit, mind, and body. In their artful approach to life and death they revealed that healing continues even while death is near at hand, that spiritual healing does not cease as the body breaks down. And their Catholic belief took them one step further by teaching that unfinished healing could continue after death through purgations of the spirit in a purifying place known as purgatory.

Medieval images of purgatory were that of a temporary hell, hardly a comfort to the dying souls who wanted to receive as much indulgence as possible from God in the judgment of their lives. But we have a different religious imagination in our time, and it's easier to imagine that purgatory is less punishment than perhaps rehabilitation for some sinful characteristics we failed to correct in our lifetime. We know more about religious beliefs other than our own than our predecessors did. In some traditions, for example, the belief in reincarnation serves much the same purpose as our purgatory: a way to continue to amend our lives until we "get it right." In reincarnation, a soul returns and gets another go at life. In Catholicism, rather than coming back, we hold the belief that we move on, with a stop—another station if you will—in a kind of halfway house for souls in need of further treatment. We might go a step further as we imagine these beliefs, and view it less as punishment, less as a "correctional" facility for wayward souls, and more as a hospital or retreat center for the treatment of chronic or acute sin. If we change our thinking into needing to care for our souls, needing medicine, needing attending physicians of the soul, then we can also loosen the hold of old images on our imaginations as well. If we think of purgatory as a place to become well enough to continue on further in our spiritual journey, we may better be able to embrace the idea of heal-ing continuing after death. Purgatory might even be a kind of intensive retreat where the only thing we pay attention to is our spiritual well-being. Nothing else matters.

If we begin to attend to our spiritual life with care and concern before death, and if we help others do the same, then we will be well on our way to living well and dying well, with perhaps a very indulgent and graceful welcome from God.

The *art* of dying well, the great gem of wisdom awaiting our reclama-tion from this spirituality from another time, teaches us that throughout our entire lives, even while we are dying and our bodies fail us, we contin-ue to be healed and made whole by our faith. Faith, like breath, is essential to our souls.

We are assisted by companions in this world who remind us of and point us to Christ who is ever with us, to his mother Mary, who comforts us, to the Father who loves us, and to the Holy Spirit who grants us peace and strength. Together with the Holy Trinity and Mary, who we have so long petitioned as Catholics to be present "now and at the hour of our death," we also look to the whole communion of saints who intercede for us from their places in the heavenly realm, so that we may arrive at the threshold of eternal life with our essence, our faith, and our spirits having experienced as much healing and wholeness as we have been capable of receiving.

If faith, then, is the ground of all healing, if its presence is as integral to life and health as breath, then it should come as no surprise that the first crisis where death or major loss comes into view is one that strikes at faith itself. Saint Paul reminds all disciples in his Epistle to the Ephesians (6:10–12) that we struggle not with flesh and blood in times of great crisis, but with powers and forces of a spiritual nature. In tough times it is not uncommon to begin to doubt not only God's love but also his very existence, and to wrestle with our faith. Therefore, our first stop in our pilgrimage through the tradition of the *Ars Moriendi* is at the station called the Crisis of Faith.

The great sixteenth-century Spanish mystic and Doctor of the Church, Saint John of the Cross, called the loss of faith the "dark night of the soul." Many others who have walked down this path of emptiness and seeming abandonment by God consider Saint John's descriptive phrase as very accurate. For in this darkness God truly seems to have vanished, and faith shatters and splinters in the abyss without a sliver of hope. Or so it seems. But Saint John does more than describe the darkness of the crisis, he also points his readers, including his present-day companions, toward the light—the outcome of the crisis—where faith not only survives but thrives. Saint John was a Carmelite priest. Because he sought a more disciplined rule of life for the monastics of his order, he made enemies within the order itself. At one point, he was imprisoned in a cell where only a spark of light pierced the hot, musty darkness of his confinement. Nevertheless, John held onto his faith, even in his darkest hour—which, for him was both a literal and a spiritual reality. Guided by that spark of light, John read his prayers daily, and what is even more astounding, he wrote spiritual poetry, poetry that to this day is considered among the finest ever to emerge from Spain. He bore witness to the strength of faith in order to survive within the crisis and to form a thriving spiritual life with even greater depth after the crisis had passed. His solution was simple: prayer. He relied on prayer in order to be able to love—to love in the crisis, out of the crisis, and to love as Jesus taught us to love. The books on prayer by Saint John of the Cross remain spiritual classics, and his stature as a wisdom figure in Christian tradition is as relevant to spiritual pilgrims today as it was in his own time. He gives us a taste of holy living and holy dying. For his best work was borne within spiritual and temporal crises and enabled him to live well, and when the time came, to die well. He teaches us how to do the same.

• • •

Sometimes the crisis of faith is triggered in the one place where the people of God expect to find solace in their brokenness—the Church. This is an area that cries out for pastoral and community responses that foster the spirit of God within the community, the Spirit that gives life, rather than the letter of the law, which kills the Spirit, as Saint Paul cautioned the Corinthian church (2 Corinthians 3:6). People seeking God, seeking healing, seeking community and wholeness, sometimes find their quest thwarted by the very church they turn to for healing. This can happen as a result of a life crisis such as a divorce, or a so-called vocational crisis when a priest seeks permission to leave active ministry in order to marry, or when adults realize their sexual orientation makes them less than welcome in the church of their heritage. In these cases, semantics are used to disguise the depth of the blow to the human spirit, a spirit already standing in brokenness. People are told they are "welcome," and yet, they are denied participation in the sacramental life of the Church if they have allowed their hearts to "rule their heads," if they have chosen to try a second time at love, marriage, work, or other life commitments. Their status is called "irregular," a cold and empty word that belies the pain inflicted by it. Or, they may participate sacramentally if they first accept their due humiliation, which is usually in addition to the painful situation they already find themselves in, stymied by the needs and desires of the heart (needs of wholeness, or *holiness*), or simply the penalty inflicted for the perceived crime of human love, or the failure of human love. It is no wonder that people who have entered through the doors of our churches seeking the face of God, and who have been met with exclusion and other forms of ostracism, would find their faith lying in pieces around them, wondering if in fact God exists at all. Where is faith, if, as it seems, the sons and daughters of the Church employ, support, or even worse, keep silent in the face of such demeaning treatment? These are truly crises of faith that affect the body of Christ as whole, and which require prayer, discernment, courage, and the support of communities of faith willing to reach out with love and the healing power of Christ.

Another way in which the Church may be the source of a crisis of faith is in the use of legal tactics, tactics common enough in the secular world for handling conflict or crisis, but which are not befitting the followers of the Gospel of Christ. Again, we can turn to Saint Paul for guidance, and again, Paul is referring to the Corinthian church when he writes:

> When any of you has a grievance against another, do you dare to take it to court before the unrighteous [that is, to the secular court, the separation of church and state, and allow a non-Christian process and judgment to be threatened or carried out], instead of taking it before the saints? Do you not know that the saints will judge the world? And if the world is to be judged by you, are you incompetent to try trivial cases? Do you not know that we are to judge angels—to say nothing of ordinary matters? If you have ordinary cases, then, do you appoint as judges those who have no standing in the church? *I say this to your*

shame. Can it be that there is no one among you wise enough to decide between one believer and another, but a believer goes to court against a believer—and before unbelievers at that?

In fact, to have lawsuits at all with one another is already a defeat for you. Why not rather be wronged? Why not rather be defrauded? *But you yourselves wrong and defraud—and believers at that* (1 Corinthians 6:1–8, emphasis added).

One can hear Paul's indignation in this passage, his incredulity at the way in which Christians are treating one another. Some problems are still with us two millennia later. And they cause the faith of good Christian women and men to falter and stumble. Sometimes, these crises extinguish the light of faith from the soul of others. We must not take part in such behavior toward one another, no matter how persuasive those who argue for legal tactics might be. The times when matters must be solved by secular courts must be seen as grand exceptions, not readily acceptable practices. In our very litigious society, listen to the radical words of Paul when he says, "Why not rather be wronged? Why not rather be defrauded?" This seems outlandish at first glance. Yet so does the gospel of Christ to those who do not believe. This is truly turning the other cheek, rather than responding in kind. It changes everything. The dynamics of conflict are totally upended if we take Paul's spiritual direction to heart. And yet, the juridical personality of the Church, honed at other times in history, in spite of ancient directives against it, has not fully given way to the pastoral heart of Vatican II and the vision of Blessed John the XXIII. Because it exists institutionally, it is difficult to teach the radical nature of the Gospel response to the People of God. Instead, one's faith is shaken if ever we have the misfortune to be dealt a legal blow for our voices, our "irregularities," or if ever a conflict with a sister or brother, or within a work of ministry, should occur.

Jesus, too, had something to say about the courts and offered suggestions as to how his disciples must act:

> So when you are offering your gift at the altar, if you remember that your brother or sister has something against you, leave your gift there before the altar and go; first be reconciled to your brother or sister, and then come and offer your gift. Come to terms quickly with your accuser while you are on the way to court with him, or your accuser may hand you over to the judge, and the judge to the guard, and you will be thrown into prison (Matthew 5: 23-25).

Be warned, Jesus is saying. Don't do this. Don't take these actions. Rather settle, reconcile, and then receive the gift of Christ's presence in communion. These teachings to put aside our anger and seek reconciliation rather than retaliation, vindictiveness, and ego-driven punitive measures, are hard to live by. Yet live them we must try to do, if we are to live well and to die at peace. And so we pray everywhere and always, for God's will and strength in our lives.

THE FINAL CRISIS: DEATH

When the crisis of faith is physical death, those who are facing death may find the idea of assisted suicide a real temptation. Why suffer? Why endure? The mystery of suffering remains just that—a mystery. The Hebrew wisdom figure, Job, was a man well acquainted with the mystery of suffering. He became so intimate with it in fact that he *could* live with it and endure it. He could live, rather than just exist in suffering. Once Job had come to a sort of acceptance, however painful, of his suffering, then miracles started taking place, and eventually his life was restored to peace and well-being. But at some point, Job also died. He chose to allow God to decide the time and circumstance of his natural death. He did not choose the ultimate act of control that would end his suffering—suicide. Instead he lived, perhaps only hanging onto a thread of existence with each new dawn, but he chose the preciousness of life over the act of taking his own life.

Self-destruction can take many forms, rather than just an outright act of final destruction. Many people who suffer emotional, mental, or physical pain choose indirect methods of assisting in their own demise. When faith is absent, it's possible to turn to anything that can alter our moods and provide some relief. Addictions are ripe for the picking when faith is teetering on the razor's edge. So a slow death, a decline, a checking out of life in one way or another becomes a habit, and eventually it may hold us in an iron grip. Then either the bottom of this self-destructive plunge comes into view and demands that a choice between life or death be made, or death sneaks in with every opportunity. We often call those "accidents," even if we choose the path most likely to produce a disaster.

Suicide can be the ultimate defiance of a God we claim we no longer believe exists, the ultimate passive-aggressive act to punish others and get back at this nonexistent God, who deserves to be thwarted by our defiance.

In fact, there are those today who have taken this wonderful spirituality of holy dying, this peaceful tradition of transformation and healing, and have misappropriated it to suggest that "dying well" means to choose when and how to die. In this warped view of wisdom, a source of peace is misinterpreted to justify violence toward oneself. Assisted suicide. It is an ultimate reaction to death, but not what the spiritual mentors whose wisdom we ply here ever intended. Rather, we believe in the Holy Spirit, the Lord, the Giver of Life!

· ❀ ·

WOODCUT 1B
INSPIRATION TO FAITH

" A T THE LEFT OF THE BED an angel displays a scroll with the words, 'Sis firmus in fide.' At Moriens' feet three discomfited devils writhe and say, 'Fugiamus victi sumus,' and 'Frustra laboravimus.' In the background a troop of the blessed, with God the Father, Our Lord, Our Lady, and Moses in the front rank, has come to console Moriens."[2] This glorious scene of comfort and care, of God holding back nothing, is gracious reassurance to Moriens that he is loved and desired in the company of the holy.

Remedy:
Inspiration to Faith

So faith comes from what is heard,
and what is heard comes through the word of Christ.

ROMANS 10:17

. . .

What, then, is the "remedy," as our forebearers called it, to the loss or potential loss of faith? What is the response to this very real and predictable stage of the journey of life, loss, and death?

The *Ars Moriendi* writers and artists warned that the crises experienced in facing death or major loss were of an unequaled nature in severity. That makes sense: when our existence seems meaningless or is threatened, we face something far beyond the realm of other crises and temptations. To remedy such times of crisis, the spirituality of the *Ars Moriendi* insisted that we learn and *practice* the art of holy dying while we are well so that when we face hardship and eventually our own death, we have the spiritual muscles to meet the crisis.

The first part of the remedy to the loss of faith, and to all of the spiritual crises, is the practice of living well. If we live well and holy, we are able to die well—a peaceful life and death. We cannot expect to die well if we have lived poorly.

We live well when we face life on life's terms, when we do not shirk our responsibilities, our vocations, or our own crises. We are responsible for how our choices affect the course of our lives, and for how they affect others. That is not to suggest that we make our decisions based on what others want from us or expect from us, but rather that we take full responsibility for our choices, even if they mean that we disappoint some people in our lives, even if we say no to the expectations of others in order to be true to ourselves and to the ways in which God may be calling us to live out our lives. We are responsible to develop our gifts and to share them, for the gifts of God are never meant to be hidden away or horded for ourselves. They are only truly fruitful within our own lives when we give them generously to the world around us. If we have gifts of music, then the music must be heard. If we are artists, then there must be those who see and hear our works. If we are teachers, we must have students. If we are scholars, we must have intellectual communities that nurture and support us. If we are mothers and fathers we must parent our children with love and as much wisdom as we are able to gather. And we must share what we gain in experience with others.

Likewise, if we suffer, we must share the gift of suffering. We must take our pain out of the closet and give it sunlight where it can become far less fearsome and far more a mysterious diamond in the rough. The Cross of Christ was not hidden from the view of the disciples, though many chose to run from its sight. What's more, the suffering and death of Christ was not something that could be contained in a tomb. Christ burst forth from his resting place in resurrection and in power, that we too might form ourselves into his likeness—fearlessly seeking Christ who bears our suffering and grants us his own strength.

For those who feel suffering must be stoically hidden away, consider the Cross of Christ, and the plight of the disciples on Good Friday. Even the disciples hid in fear, but it was not to last. The Easter experience brought them out-of-doors, into the light, and gave hope.

And in the in-between times, they gathered and prayed. They lamented and mourned. They experienced the range of spiritual crises. But we know the end of the story: Christ rose. The Holy Spirit came with tongues of fire and with all the gifts of the Spirit to enable them to live, to live well, and to die with peace and courage no matter whether they died as martyrs or died in their sleep. Faith won the day, and will win our day as well, if we crack the door open for the messengers of hope, who, like Mary Magdalene and Mary the disciple of Christ, are knocking at the door of our own pain and our own crisis, with good news of great joy, if we will only come and see. See the empty tomb, and turn in prayer to Christ who is as much with us now as he was in the garden on that Easter morning with Mary Magdalene, his cherished disciple. If we turn, if we pray, if we seek the Spirit of God, we will find Christ is in all situations, in all times, and will never leave us. Listen to the stories of the saints, the stories of faith in your own communities, and the stories held in the treasure trove of Scripture. Listen, and hear the words of faith ensconced in prayer.

．　．　．

In the spring of 2001 I had the privilege of attending a pilgrimage in Chicago for those whose lives had been touched by breast cancer. They came to a Sunday liturgy in May that had been specially designed for them, and it included the anointing of the sick for these pilgrims, most of whom were women. A procession of these women, ranging in age from the unexpectedly young to octogenarians, came forward at the appointed time to be anointed by the Church and receive prayer for healing. It was a procession of courage and faith. Tears flowed and smiles emerged. Some were in the midst of treatment, others were counting the years of remission. All shared a bond not only of a common crisis but of a common faith.

Two women were invited forward at the time of the homily to give witness to their crisis and their faith. One of these women was very young, too young it seemed to have suffered from such an illness. Both women were mothers who worried for their children's comfort and peace during the cancer treatment, and both prayed to be able to live long enough to see their children grow up.

The women had far more to say about faith in Christ than they had to say about the trauma and trials of a life-threatening illness. They emphasized the role of prayer in their lives at the time of diagnosis, surgery, and chemotherapy. They spoke of the healing words received from pastoral caregivers and support groups. They returned again and again to words of hope borne of faith, and faith borne of prayer. They said they had taken their illness and given it to Jesus. They allowed Jesus to take it, worry about it, and care for them.

And there they were, survivors, sharing their stories with the whole community, not asking for sympathy but *giving* away the gift of hope with generosity and remarkable faith.

Their witness talks were followed after the Sunday liturgy by a gathering for yet another speaker. Again a very young and very beautiful woman shared her story of breast cancer, peppering her reflections with counsel and wisdom for those who now walk the same path. This woman spoke of not only the trauma of the illness but of well-meaning friends and acquaintances who, not knowing what to say or do, often reacted in ways that were harmful to her well-being. How does one keep faith when family and friends either flee the crisis or act thoughtlessly? Most devastating of all, this young woman faced the breakup of her marriage as a result of the disease, an illness her husband could not bear to live with. To add such trauma to the illness itself seemed more than even Job of the Hebrew Scriptures could bear—such enormous loss, such pain, such uncertainty that one would even live to see another year. And yet, this woman was living well. She was standing before us in courage and with peace, eager to share her story in the event that it could help someone else, and give others strength and hope. Most significantly, she shared her faith. Faith was the cornerstone of her survival, of forgiveness, and of carrying on with the gift of life with each new day given.

These women have learned to live well, in faith, and they publicly shared the gift of faith, nurtured through what arguably could be called the gift of crisis. For where else but in crises do these remarkable stories appear?

It would have been easy for these women to descend into bitterness, anger, and hopelessness in the face of their illness. But they did not. With prayer, with a community of support, and with faith that could move mountains, they live well. In fact, they live sanctified lives in our midst.

The keynote speaker told us at the end of her talk that she had just been told the cancer had returned and was at a very advanced state. Nevertheless, she was on a pilgrimage, bearing witness to the power of faith. She was meeting the crisis in wisdom and in the power of the Holy Spirit. We have a remarkable God.

•   •   •

The spiritual crisis of faith may surface when we face the death of a loved one, or when we are diagnosed with a serious illness ourselves. It may arise when we doubt ourselves, when our self-worth dwindles in the face of hardship, or when a cherished relationship shatters and we are helpless to change things. It may appear when a promising career crumbles through forces beyond our control. And sometimes it creeps in as a result of our own choices, our own failings or neglect: what we have done and what we have failed to do. During these times, faith lies silent in a room within our mind that resembles more a tomb than an interior chapel where we can go to meet God.

Remember, then, what the tomb of Jesus symbolized, for the resurrection is our symbol and our hope as well. The tomb of Jesus became a place of wonderment and elation. But it first had to serve as a tomb.

It is helpful to remember during the times we bury our faith that tombs are placed on hallowed ground, and that where death is laid to rest the resting place is sacred space. These images may help us see why the

Passion of Christ was so central to the prayers and meditations of the early practitioners of the art of holy dying; for Christ, too, experienced the depths of darkness when he prayed in the Garden of Gethsemane and again when he cried out from the cross in utter abandonment. Christ experienced all these things so that he may be the source of our healing and transformation. We know and believe that Christ rose from the dead, emerged from that tomb, and continues to embrace his followers in all times and in all places, with a peace that surpasses human understanding.

The art of holy living and dying recognized that at times when faith is lost, "missing in action," so to speak, despair can set in and a person might consider suicide as a very real option. Losing faith is no minor crisis. It is the conviction that God does not exist, that there is no reason to continue.

Have you ever felt like dying? The pain of a major life crisis can be so great that we cry out for relief, and if the pain is great enough, we may actually "feel like dying." We are not ourselves during those times. We need the strong support of prayer and the support of those who have themselves walked through the fire.

Sometimes when I actually tell people portions of my life story, they are amazed, because they will say to me, "You don't look like you've been through all that," and I know that that can only be because of God. They ask me how I have not only survived but seem to have much to give. My answer is as simple as it is mysterious. The answer is faith. The answer is God. Even my therapist has asked me to explain how I came out okay from these experiences. From a childhood of great neglect and the tragedy of an extended family wracked with alcoholism—and with all the life wreckage that comes with it—to my own adult crises, such as my brief, tormented marriage to another alcoholic, as predictable as the rain for someone with a family history like my own. The marriage produced a beautiful son, but it also caused me to flee from domestic violence with only a duffel bag of belongings to call my own. During those difficult months, I faced the very real prospect of raising my son alone, with no child support (indeed that was the case in the years to come), and no family support to speak of. My parents were dead. (Their early deaths were, no doubt, linked to alcohol abuse.) We were on our own. Or so I thought. This experience shattered my childlike faith and caused me to wonder about all those questions we ask of God when horrible things have befallen us. Where is God? How could a loving God have allowed this to happen? What have I done wrong? How could I have ended up in such a horrendous situation? Why was God punishing me?

The first thing I learned was that I was *not alone.* I turned to my community of faith, who were very much there for me. I sought help. I was surrounded by friends who all had one thing in common: faith in Christ. Prayers and support from other Christians encouraged me and my young son, and kept us in a bond of love. I formed what is known as a "family of choice," and have continued to form these relationships when I have moved to new communities for my work or my education. It has been many years now since I boarded a plane with my baby and a bag of clothes for the two of us, heading for a few months of sleeping on couches while I tried to regain control of my life. Faith kept us in God's care, and faith allows me to tell the story today, as I live now with my son who has just crossed the threshold into adulthood, and who is one of the kindest and most loving human beings I know.

In the intervening years I had to face other demons, each able to shake faith in their own ways, but all connected in the end. I had to face my own dependency on alcohol, which I had turned into a medicinal ritual each night. It had become my way of medicating the pain of my life: the single parenthood, the chronic economic stress, the loneliness. When finally set free from the addiction, by no other means than by prayer and the healing power of God, I faced an even new set of challenges: uncovering the depression that had always lurked behind the glasses of wine each night. I never even knew I was depressed! I'll say more about my depression later, but for now, let me simply join the chorus of gratitude from those who have found faith in the dark nights of the soul. The darkness becomes a gift, if we keep our hearts receptive long enough to receive it.

· · ·

Sometimes our hearing and our sight is so blocked that we find ourselves on our deathbed before we are willing to turn to God. Deathbed conversions were very common occurrences in medieval times when the *Ars Moriendi* handbooks first appeared. It was hoped that those who used the handbooks to help others would gradually learn and be transformed and that they themselves would be so affected as to avoid a deathbed conversion and be able to enjoy a life lived well during times of health.

Deathbed conversions seize us unprepared. Just as the wisdom of our own time teaches us to get our affairs in order so that our families are not left with unnecessary burdens and other crises we have created, the art of holy living and dying also advises us to prepare ourselves spiritually. This Christian tradition of faith challenges us to become people of character and strength who can meet the crisis of faith with courage and tenacity. How is that accomplished? We have already said that prayer is the key. But prayer is also something that must be learned and practiced. It is a discipline of life. And so, we accomplish living well and dying well *by discipline*. All true artists are disciplined in their craft. And art and craft are exactly the words that are used in the *Ars Moriendi* books to describe what holy living and holy dying is all about. To learn these holy ways is to learn a craft, or an art form. *Discipline* is also the same word from which we derive the term "disciple." If we are disciples of Christ, we must be disciplined, for that is what Jesus himself taught and expected. We should not be surprised that living well and dying well require a practice that involves spiritual disciplines or exercises. In a culture that obsesses over firm abs and toned bodies, we know that physical toning requires work. All the more for the health of the spirit and soul, which will not fail us when the body does.

In the same way that a person who works out will be faithful to their exercise—whether at a health club, on a bike path, running several miles a week, or getting up each morning and practicing yoga—a person who is spiritually fit will also faithfully engage in practices that help to strengthen their spiritual muscles and tone their lives so they may proceed each day with their priorities straight, grounded in the peace of Christ. Prayer is a spiritual practice, or exercise, and it comes in many forms, as does its kissing cousin, meditation.

Prayer and meditation, then, are the essential ingredients for maintaining proper spiritual and mental health. To go without prayer is as hazardous to your "whole" health as to go without eating is to your physical health. Prayer and meditation need to be a priority, a "first things first" event in our daily lives. Nutritionists tell us that breakfast is the most important meal of the day. It's a "first thing," a breaking of the fast of sleep, when we took in no physical nourishment.

Imagine that our souls go through a similar process. If we have not properly nourished our souls, then our spiritual nature must rely on past nourishment, which is insufficient to the current day's needs. We need our daily prayer. Setting aside time in the morning for prayer is very wise but it's also very tough. It is so much easier to hit the snooze button for a few more winks of sleep before getting ready for the day's schedule. Significantly, breakfast and prayer are so easily sacrificed in favor of sleep, or spending a few minutes at the computer screen surfing the net before heading off to work, or making a quick phone call. Sleep is good, right? We are bombarded by reports saying Americans don't get enough sleep. On the other hand, we are a nation that is collectively overweight, according to study after study, so what's wrong with skipping breakfast? A little nutritional information can answer that question. And a shift in priorities might solve the sleep problem and present us with time to pray as well. This isn't easy. In order to live well, spiritual care means forming new habits—the old ones don't give up without a fight. But you'll be delighted with the results, if you give it a go on your own, before your health care providers start recommending it.

The Eucharist is *the* premier spiritual exercise, and to live well, we must not neglect the coming together for the Lord's Supper. We sing, we pray, we hear the Word of God, and we take and eat the body of Christ, and take and drink of the blood of Christ. This is our faith, and this is how we practice it for our own benefit, and for the good of others whom we are called to love and serve as members of Christ's body. Remember that the Eucharist is the only sacrament that is both part of our Christian initiation, and at the same time, a sacrament that we come to over and over again all our lives. We are initiated into Christianity to make this remarkable, recurring feast possible—a never-ending feast of the body and blood of Christ, present among us and within us each time we gather for the Eucharist.

Every time we come to the eucharistic banquet we are meditating upon the Passion of Christ, and the Passion of Christ is the central theme of the *Ars Moriendi.* To live well and to die well, we keep the Cross of Christ always before us. We stand in awe of so great a sacrifice, and we reverently enter into memorial with each rendering of the eucharistic prayer that transforms the ordinary into the extraordinary substance of life. Here is Christ, in whom we "live and move and have our being" (Acts 17:28). Alleluia!

The exercise of our eucharistic calling and privilege receives pride of place among the spiritual disciplines of the Catholic Christian and pride of place in the sacramental life. We are a sacramental people, having entered this life through baptism. We are nourished continuously throughout our lives by the eucharistic banquet set before us. Sacramental life is a life that embraces mystery, that learns to live comfortably with mystery and with the mysticism that is our tradition and the heritage of our spiritual life. Nowhere is this mystery and mysticism more dynamically witnessed than in our celebration of the Eucharist. "This is the Lamb of God, who takes away the sins of the world!" And, "Happy are those who are called to his supper!" We come to bask in the presence of Christ in these gifts and in the gift of our community, the living body of Christ. We come to hear Christ present in the Liturgy of the Word proclaimed and preached before us, another gift! And then we turn to the table and offer *our* gifts of thanksgiving and praise, and receive into our hands and mouths the gift of Christ in bread and wine. Work of human hands lifted up and broken for us, fruit of the earth poured out for us. Together with the assembly gathered, we say, "Lord I am not worthy, but only say the word and I shall be healed." We are healed by the Word, received into Christ's presence and at the same time we receive the presence of Christ into our lives—becoming one in Christ, with Christ, and through Christ. Again and again and again, Alleluia!

Spiritual direction is another exercise for living well that has come to be accepted in our own culture. An ancient tradition within the Church, this practice of regularly spending time with a spiritual companion or guide, a mentor of the spirit, has seen a welcome renewal in recent years and can be invaluable in the quest to live a holy and fulfilling life. Spiritual directors may be laypersons or ordained men or women, who have been trained in the art of direction. It is not therapy and should not be confused with psychological counseling. It is a spiritual friendship whose purpose is to help find God's presence in all things, and in the process discern the will of God in our lives.

The sacrament of penance and reconciliation is premier exercise for spiritual health. A clear conscience is irreplaceable in good spiritual health as is the ability to live in freedom and peace. Virtually all religious traditions have some form of confession within the tradition. For Catholic Christians, the sacrament of penance and reconciliation is often the fruit of good prior work done in spiritual direction. While direction helps to sort out our lives and gives us a safe place to do so, the sacrament is where we go to sacramentalize our stories, confess our faults, and seek forgiveness, relief, and guidance in making amends for our wrongdoing or for what we have failed to do—our neglect. In the sacrament we seek spiritual medicine, the well-known relief of facing up to our defects and sins and naming them, out loud, to another human being, and doing so in the context of absolute confidentiality and in prayer. This sacrament is truly one of the greatest gifts of our Catholic heritage. Practicing it can bring a new world of understanding of grace and the sacramental nature of our lives. Penance and reconciliation are like the visit to the doctor. Every once in a while we need to go. When there is grave sin, we need to seek out the sacrament as soon as possible. When there are lesser sins, we can rely on the Eucharist to heal and nourish us, or we can make our annual pilgrimages to reconciliation rooms or confessionals, or we can make appointments for the sacrament. Sometimes, if we haven't availed ourselves of the sacrament in many years, we may want to truly scrutinize our lives, using a written examination that helps us remember the inventory of our lives. We take stock, bringing it to the confessor who, in representing Christ and the Church on earth, acts as a physician of the soul to assist us through this healing process. Don't neglect this practice. It is a gem in the sacramental crown of the Church.

Spiritual reading is yet another spiritual exercise that can benefit our lives as Christians. It can take the form of meditative reading of Scripture, through the tradition of *Lectio Divina*, which, simply put, means reading Scripture as prayer and meditation. There are books that can help you master this method, and retreats and workshops to open up this practice for those who are unfamiliar with it.

Spiritual reading is also the reading of good spiritual literature: the lives of the saints, for example, or books of prayers and meditations, books that recount contemporary stories of faith, and books that present faith through fiction, through theological study, or through biography.

This is exactly what the early practitioners of the *Ars Moriendi* tradition did: they told stories, they read the stories out loud to one another, and they gazed on the pictorial depictions of the stories if they could not read. We don't have to have difficulty reading to want to avail ourselves of Christian art as a meditation tool. Art, too, is a form of spiritual "reading" and exercise. Just as the woodcuts presented in this book helped sixteenth-century Europeans form their consciences, live their faith, and help one another to die well, so too, can we gaze upon the Passion of Christ in art, the stories of the saints in stained glass windows, the stations of the cross in our local churches, the classic works of art in books, museums, and private collections, and all other manner of Christian art, contemporary and classic, in order to be strengthened and enlarged in our faith.

Retreats and days of prayer or recollection are another spiritual exercise available not only at special centers but also in local parishes and at pilgrimage sites. Going on a retreat is a wonderfully healthy practice for the good of our souls. What's more, that which makes us healthy, that strengthens us, that heals us and makes us more honest and free, filters back into our own families and communities as a gift to others as well. If you can't make a three-day retreat, make a day of recollection, or day of prayer. It usually consists of speakers presenting meditations and offering a time for reflection, spiritual direction, or other forms of spiritual care. If you can't do a full day, do a half day. If you can't do a half day, find time and space in your own home to "retreat," to experience solitude, to rest, and to engage in prayerful activities, such as reading, listening to sacred music, or making sacred art.

Community is also a spiritual practice, and is essential to the art of living well and dying well. Community must be practiced, or it simply will not exist in our lives. If we neglect community we won't have the gift that is there for us, and we will deprive the community of our presence and our gifts. Community is so significant that it is safe to put all the previously mentioned spiritual exercises on one side of the Remedy to the Crisis page and place community on the other side, as a large and essential category of its own. As Catholics our tradition is deeply communal. In the *Ars Moriendi*, community is the life of the art.

One of our spiritual tasks in this time of great independence and selfishness is to accept that we cannot go through life alone, at least not if we expect to live well. Life is a communal enterprise. To reclaim this tenant of our Catholic heritage we must be willing to be *present* to one another—to give and receive love. Especially in times of crisis, we must surround and be surrounded by others in love, presence, prayers, and hope. One of our best contemporary models of this communal *remedy* can be found in the practice of Twelve-Step groups. No one goes it alone. The group supports, prays for, and walks with the person. A sponsor commits to a one-on-one relationship of spiritual companionship and assistance, a very serious commitment. A sponsor in a Twelve-Step group is very much like a spiritual director in Christian understanding. In fact, the desert anchorites of early Christianity, who birthed the practice of spiritual direction, also used the word sponsor to describe the role of the director. A sponsor in a Twelve-Step program is a spiritual cousin of our traditional Christian roles of confessor, spiritual fathers and mothers, and physicians of the soul. In the history of the Christian tradition those particularly gifted in the area of soul work are discerned within a community and trained in the art of spiritual direction. It will be very helpful at the time of a crisis of faith if one already has a spiritual companion. If not, waste no time in finding this sponsor, guide, or mentor. The Irish call this person a soul friend, or *anam cara*.

· · ·

The early *Ars Moriendi* practitioners knew the importance of this spiritual guide in living well and dying well. As in our own time, the practitioners also faced a shortage of ordained clergy, so the expectation was that the laity would learn and practice the art of holy dying and they, in turn, would accompany one another in the journey to death. The priest would arrive, whenever possible, for the final sacraments and for the scrutinies. The *Ars* required that pastoral scrutinies be performed, much as we have the practice of scrutinies in the third, fourth, and fifth Sundays of Lent for catechumens who are proceeding through the Rite of Christian Initiation of Adults. The scrutinies for the dying person were the final round, the last inventory of one's life, the final cleansing and confession. The spiritual director may be an ordained priest or a trained and gifted layperson. The confessor for the sacrament of penance and reconciliation is, of course, a priest, but the companions of the dying person may simply be those who hear with ears of the heart.

There is a strong narrative base to the remedy for the loss of faith and a strong voice to the remedy for the "voice of sickness." The local community, both ordained and lay, as well as the family—indeed all the people of God—"practiced" the art of holy dying by being with the dying person and praying with them, telling them stories of the ancient people of faith, and sharing their own stories, performing the narrative together.

Two spiritual medicines that should be applied liberally in response to the loss of faith are prayer and storytelling. In other words, we need liturgy—whether in the home, in a hospital, or in a church sanctuary.

Remember that liturgy is the "work of the people," for that is the literal meaning of the word. It is our work, all of us. Liturgy is not just the celebration of the Eucharist, or other sacraments, it also encompasses prayer services, healing services, and other communal gatherings of prayer and solace. There are liturgies of lamentation for those who suffer or grieve, and ultimately there is a funeral liturgy that we can help create with our shared vision and concern.

Readings from Scripture, prayer from tradition, and prayers and stories written and told for the occasion are performed in a communal manner. A liturgy of lamentation, a cry to God for restoration of faith, for healing, and for mercy may be appropriate. Psalms and hymns that speak of bewilderment, anger, and hopelessness are all appropriate expressions of lamentation.

Intercession is another integral form of prayer. We pray for one another. We ask for healing. We bring our needs before the Lord. We widen and deepen the intercessory action of the Church as a whole whenever we engage in a eucharistic liturgy. But most of all, through all of these works of the people, and all these liturgies, we do not go it alone. Companions and watchers surround the suffering persons and weave for them, culled from stories and prayers, a tapestry of comfort.

The most effective scriptures for these rituals are those that recount the lives of the great pillars of faith throughout history: Moses, Abraham, Jacob, Job, Ruth, and Rahab, along with Mary, the Virgin Mother of God, the apostles, martyrs, confessors, and all the saints who have pleased God. Hearing these stories helps to renew our faith and our baptismal vows. Through these stories we are brought to prayer to our Father and Creator. In the New Testament, readings from the Letter to the Hebrews will remind us of faith, and the Gospels will remind us of the teachings of Jesus over and over again. At the time of spiritual crisis, we need repetition. We need the faith of others to restore our own faith but also we need the faith of others to shore up our own faith even once it is restored. We need to hear and hang onto the ministry of the Word, when our minds are not clear and our bodies are weak.

We pray together. Our forebearers chose the Nicene Creed as a fundamental prayer to pray with the person enduring the crisis of faith. This is our faith! The words we hear at baptisms come back to us anew: "This is our faith. This is the faith of the Church. We are proud to profess it, in Christ Jesus, our Lord." The more deeply we go into the crisis of faith, the more we come back to our baptism. Baptismal vows are renewed in the sacrament of penance and reconciliation, and they are reflected in the funeral rite. In the funeral rite the symbols of baptism are prominently in view. Consider how in death, the final crisis having been met, the community gathers to continue its works of prayer, and to continue to evoke the importance of baptism and life in the Spirit culminating in rituals of death and final committal. The first step in the funeral rite is the reception of the body. At the entrance to the church, just as in baptism, the body is received. This is the place where the sacramental life of the deceased began: at the entrance to the church, the entryway into the community, with baptism and the support of the community. The Church is where the Christian life has been publicly nourished through the Eucharist, through the Word of God, and through other sacramental rituals such as confirmation, penance and reconciliation, and perhaps marriage or holy orders. The symbol of the church sanctuary is very great—it symbolizes life in Christ and life in the Christian community.

During the rite of reception the coffin is sprinkled with holy water, signifying once again, baptism. It is then customary in many communities to drape a funeral pall over the coffin, a white cloth that calls to mind the white garment bestowed at baptism. Again and again in our sacramental lives, we are called back to our baptism, our initiation into Christ and into the Christian community. Then there is a procession to the front of the Church for the funeral liturgy. At the end of the liturgy there occurs another reminder of baptism in the form of the Final Commendation and Farewell. Here, the community acknowledges that as we are all called to live in Christ through baptism, we all share the same destiny of death, and the hope of the resurrection with Christ. Prayer continues—always; the member of the body of Christ who has suffered and died is surrounded by prayer. Once again, there may be another sprinkling rite, as more holy water is cast upon the coffin, concluding the funeral liturgy with yet another reminder of baptism and of eternal life with Christ. Incense may also be a part of the ritual. The incensing of the body reminds us that our bodies are the temple of the Holy Spirit. Incense signifies prayer, respect, and the sacredness of the human body. Cradle to grave, we invite sacramental rites into our lives to mark each beginning and each end with the greatest dignity and holiness.

Several years ago I attended the funeral of a colleague from the radio station where I worked. I seemed to be the only other Catholic in the group, so I found myself being asked all sorts of questions as the funeral liturgy took place. Most significantly, everyone wanted to know about the holy water and the incense, and the mystery of holy communion. "What does it mean?" "What does all this ritual mean?" they asked. I explained, and understood better myself, that the water and the incense, the bread and the wine all signified life. They mean living as well as we can and dying well because we have been attentive to our lives in Christ. They mean we have not gone through life alone. We are members each of the body of Christ.

· · ·

And so at this time in our pilgrimage, perhaps the final pilgrimage for the person who is sick or fatally injured, we make the *confession of faith*. The words we have spoken Sunday after Sunday throughout our lives, are presented anew at the time of crisis. "We believe." We recite the creed. The ancients knew this was a strengthening exercise, and so we learn from those who have gone before us, and we confess our faith as well. Confessing faith helps to renew our faith.

When we have confessed what we believe, we recite the Lord's Prayer, as Jesus taught us. We then pray the prayers left to us by holy women and men. The prayer of Saint Francis: Let us be instruments of peace even in death. Even in crisis. We ask the intercession of Mary, who, without flinching, accompanied her Son in meeting his unjust death. To Mary we offer the request that she be present, "*now* and at the hour of our death." If we have been raised in the Catholic Church, we have recited those words from childhood. Now we understand more deeply why it is that Mary is beseeched at the hour of our death, for we do indeed call on her for intercession and accompaniment. We seek the intercession of the saints. If the dying person is too sick to speak the words of prayer themselves, we simply look for what assent they can give. Can the sick person, the wounded person, the person in crisis at least say Amen? Good enough. Can the person so weak from sickness manage to squeeze your hand? Wonderful! Can the friend wracked with the emotional pain of a personal crisis manage to give a nod of their head? This is all it takes. If even these signals of joining in prayer are not possible, we do not give up. We then call upon our own faith all the more intensely to intercede for them. The invitation is always extended to lean on the prayers and faith of others if they cannot muster their own faith.

The handbooks of five hundred years ago admonished those who would pray to do so with strong voices. Think about this. No weak voices allowed. Save your weeping for another time. Now is the time for strong voices. Strength begets strength. So, too, we can lift up our voices, we can sing, and pray with those who suffer and mourn. Loudly. Enthusiastically. With faith resounding in our voices. With belief coloring each phrase, each response, each syllable of song. Our voices are marvelous things. A voice is like a fingerprint, unique, personal, and a conveyor of emotion and thought. Our voices sometimes "give us away" when the sound we are trying to make doesn't match our inner reality. When we try desperately to sound happy when we're sad. When we try to sound confident but our voice quivers in protest. When we do not tell the truth, and our voices give subtle signals to those who are clever enough to read the signs. Our voices are remarkable indeed. So when we are commanded to pray and sing for the person in a crisis of faith with "strong voices," we know this is a very important element of caring for one another. Give away strength, with voices of courage, faith, and hope.

Our predecessors believed that sickness had its own voice. It was considered imperative for those who practiced the art of holy dying to understand this and to be able to separate the voice of the illness from the voice of the person. This is a beautiful understanding of what is occurring to the sufferer. It is also deeply compassionate. The voice of sickness, which often is a voice that is blind to the presence of God, must be countered with the strong voices of those who do indeed see God's presence, even at this time of crisis. The voice of sickness must be overcome with a great voice of faith. And so the directive: Pray with strong voices! Sing from the heart, and tell stories of faith, from Scripture and from life experience. Never be timid, but be full of faith and life. Despite what is seen in the presence of death, continue to seek healing, while nevertheless accepting the outcome. For in this crisis, where can we go to hide from God, as the psalmist tells us? We may think God is absent, but in fact the Spirit of God is so fully present that we cannot escape. King David knew this, and he cried out:

> Where can I go from your spirit?
> Or where can I flee from your presence?
> If I ascend to heaven, you are there;
> if I make my bed in Sheol, you are there.
> If I take the wings of the morning
> and settle at the farthest limits of the sea,
> even there your hand shall lead me,
> and your right hand shall hold me fast.
> If I say, "Surely the darkness shall cover me,
> and the light around me become night"
> even the darkness is not dark to you;

the night is as bright as the day,
for darkness is as light to you (Psalm 139:7-12).

The dark night of the soul for David proved to be one with the light.

. . .

The loss of faith is the first crisis named in the *Ars Moriendi*. It is the beginning of the passage of a series of crises commonly experienced by those facing death or major loss. The remedy to the crisis of faith is by a joint effort of companions in solidarity with the suffering person. We can conclude that the strong and effective medicine to overcome the temptation to the loss of faith resides in prayer, in the narratives of the faith of those who have gone before us, and within the faith of those who surround us in the present with love.

We who find ourselves in health of body and in good faith are called to accompany those who suffer and to be accompanied when we suffer. When we do this we not only live out our Christian responsibilities in the body of Christ, we also receive great benefits to our own souls. We prepare ourselves for our own deaths little by little each time we give ourselves away to others. We pray that we too will be accompanied by loving friends and family, surrounded by the communion of saints at the hour of our death.

There is always the possibility that death will come like the thief in the night of Scripture and overwhelm us. When death is a sudden event there is no time for rituals of prayer and counsel, accompaniment and solace. That is why it is all the more important for the principles of living well and dying well to be practiced while we are in good health and living full days. For when the hour of our death does arrive, we will have prepared ourselves consciously to be as ready as possible, each and every day. No one is perfect nor fully prepared, but to the extent we can be, we do well to practice this art on a daily basis for ourselves and for others.

Our pilgrimage, our stational liturgy, moves on now with a meditation and prayer before arriving at the second stop in our journey.

Meditation

(FROM THE SEVEN LAST WORDS OF JESUS)

This meditation may be prayed as a multi-voice piece, within a liturgy, or it may simply be used for solo reading and meditation.

"My God, My God, Why Have You Forsaken Me?"

Forsaken, I am an ocean of fear, vast and without horizon.
Forsaken, I sink into black, dusty waters of oblivion without notice.
Forsaken, the waves tease out my breath like a fisher of death
plunging its net around me.

The air is haunting, the night without stars, the bed of waters
masks chaos beneath its calm facade.

I scream and there is no sound—forsaken by my own reflection,
I do not exist. No evil tormentor ever dreamed a more complete devastation
than this nonexistent existence—
on this cross that does not yet complete its death-task.
My abandonment is stretched out for all to see and I am mocked.
I am proof of futility; my arms are fastened outward toward You who are not there.

Do you hear the vacant ocean?
No ship would dare to sail these waters, yet I have been adrift
where there is no compass and no hope.

In cresting shadows I cease to see form;
I am betrayed once and for all by Abba, whom I have served.

• • •

Time in and out and weaving droplets of cold fear,
the hours ice the afternoon of desolation.

Chilled hearts, frozen in fear, abandoned me in my time of need but *You!*
Father of hearts and author of life,
even *You* have turned and left me to the shame of this cross,
this humiliation of all hope, this empty, ceaseless degradation.

• • •

[*Reader: Change of voice or change readers.*]

• • •

Pray now sisters! Pray now brothers! Pray children of the most high!

Pray that you be found serving God until the end of your days.
Pray that you be found to be good and faithful servants always.
Pray that abandonment such as our Lord has suffered will take
the place of all abandonments. Suffered for us, that
we may live and move in Christ who is our perpetual light.

• • •

Fearing, we seek strong refuge in you, O God, our Father in heaven.

Trembling, we nevertheless—praise your name O God of all creation!

Halting in speech, we declare, "your kingdom come, your will be done,
on this earth, and in all heaven."

Hungry of heart, we seek the bread of life at your hands.

Trespassing, we dare to ask forgiveness at this dark hour,
and we turn and grant forgiveness to our trespassers.

Wandering, we turn to you as shepherd, and ask that you lead us
out of this crushing temptation to lose all faith.
Deliver us, O God of the abandoned ones,
God who dwells in no temple but *is* the temple of all holiness.

Deliver us O God, from this cross, from this dark night,
from this pain and utter loss. . .
nevertheless,
Not our will, but yours —
We drink the cup,
and eat the bread,
until we can no more lift our heads.

We gaze upon the abandoned one whom we love and ask your mercy,
with Him,
and in Him,
who spoke our dreams
and healed our brokenness,
and who is now broken as bread before you.

Hear our cry and lamentation even when we cannot hear ourselves.

Blessed is God, who is now and ever shall be,
world without end, Amen.

Peace of Christ be with you all . . .

R/. And also with you.

Prayer

Standing before your cross, O Christ,
steeped in the passion you endured for us
and experiencing our share of the cross,
We pray for faith.
We have lost sight of your resurrection,
and we wander in the tomb of the faithless.

We are the blind seeking sight,
and we know that you have this gift to offer!
Do not allow us to suffer as those who have no hope,
but rather shower us with rain-drenched faith,
and renew the faith instilled in us by baptism and by your grace.

Renew! Renew! Renew! is our cry and lamentation.
We have lost what once was ours,
it is in your safekeeping.
Unlock the treasures of faith, dear Savior,
and bestow upon us at this dark hour the gift of faith once again.

Allow faith to course through our veins once again, that we may
be of service to you and a witness to others
even as the light of this world ebbs for us,
and the light of your eternal world rises.

Send faith on angels' wings, Holy Spirit of Mercy,
and on the lips of those who comfort us,
That we may be whole in spirit and strong in our souls,
and that nevertheless, Your will may be done.
We pray at all times and in all places, through Christ our Lord.

Amen.

·11·
The Second
Spiritual Crisis
and Remedy

WOODCUT 2A

DESPAIR

"THE BED IS SURROUNDED by devils and those whom Moriens has wronged. 'Perjurus est,' says one fiend, pointing to the man against whom Moriens has committed perjury; 'Fornicatus est,' says another, designating the woman whom he has sexually betrayed. Others accuse him: 'Occidisti' and 'Avare vixisti,' the first for the victim of a stab wound, the second for a beggar seated in his rags beside the bed and for a naked man whom he might have clothed. In the background a devil says, 'Ecce peccata tua,' and holds up a placard on which are written his sins."[1] Who can withstand such a barrage of accusation, such convincing evidence that one has no place among the redeemed? Moriens has received the full weight of guilt heaped upon his deathbed

Crisis:
Despair

Save me, O God,
for the waters have come up to my neck.
I sink in deep mire,
where there is no foothold;
I have come into deep waters,
and the flood sweeps over me.
I am weary with my crying;
my throat is parched.
My eyes grow dim
with waiting for my God.

PSALM 69:1–3

. . .

W hen I was a child growing up in Massachusetts, the Sisters of the Presentation at Saint Patrick's School told us that to despair was a mortal sin. This was a particularly bad sin among sins, or so it seemed to my childhood ears, as it was not something you *did* so much as something you thought. To avoid the sin, we were absolutely not allowed to despair in the face of sadness and calamity, no matter how bad. To despair at the end of life, well that would mean to die in mortal sin and then there would be no way out. And you could achieve this deadly sin just by thinking your way into it. It was an attitude. A verb of thought. A powerful, gripping way of being. We stop now in our pilgrimage to ponder this crisis of despair.

There was a germ of truth to what the good sisters of my youth believed, even if they did not communicate it in the best way. Despair is

43

certainly deadening to the soul. To despair is more attitude than active crime, yet it casts our souls in stone, hardening our hearts and causing grief not only to those around us but also, as Saint Paul teaches in his letter to the Ephesians, to the Holy Spirit. Paul goes on to list a number of behaviors unbefitting for believers because they grieve God and others—ranging from foul language to bitterness, fury, shouting, and malice—and admonishes us, "do not grieve the Holy Spirit of God, with which you were marked with a seal for the day of redemption" (4:30). As we well know, heeding Paul's directive is not always easy. When we are sick and weak, we are particularly vulnerable to negative thinking. The sisters didn't quite understand that despair is not something we can turn off and on like a light switch. Overcoming despair is neither as simple as walking away from a serious temptation to engage in actions that are harmful, nor as complex as extricating ourselves from systems of injustice or unethical practices. Instead, despair is a state of mind, a spiritual malady that requires serious intervention and prayer. In fact, despair seems to turn itself on in our hearts far more easily than it is turned off. Despair grows and flourishes when our thinking is captive to negativity and our bodies are weak.

The crisis of despair is all tangled up with guilt, self-doubt, and even self-hatred, and the inability to believe that God can or will love us and receive us into his presence.

In the early *Ars Moriendi* picture books, the woodcuts depicting this crisis showed the dying person, who is called simply, Moriens, the medieval Everyman who represents death, being tormented by people from his past who have been wronged and by demons who seek to destroy all hope in Christ. Echoing through the dying person's mind are all sorts of accusations, real and imagined: the friend who was betrayed, the spouse against whom adultery was committed, the children who were neglected, and all those who had been ill-treated. Also teaming up in the deathbed assault are accusations of the sins of omission: the naked man who was ignored, the hungry who were passed by, the widows and the orphans to whom no heed was paid. Against such a mountain of evidence of unworthiness, the *Ars* asks How can the dying person retain any sense of hope that Christ will welcome the soul, receive the spirit, or embrace the faulty life of the pilgrim?

Left to our own devices, it seems unlikely that any of us could withstand an assault of guilt and unworthiness as was depicted in the *Art of Holy Dying* pictures. Despair is created in such a crisis of guilt. Today, we are just as prone to despair as our medieval predecessors. Technology cannot stop it. Financial security cannot keep it at bay. Intellect cannot overcome it. If one has not lived well, the crisis of despair will be of monumental proportions. Living well, then, is the first line of defense against being overtaken by the crisis of despair. Living well means we examine our consciences regularly, seek spiritual direction or counsel, make amends for wrongs committed, and confess our sins sacramentally when necessary. The sacrament of penance and reconciliation, where we announce our faults and sins and seek forgiveness, is a healing sacrament of mercy and spiritual care. Living well means we do not fear our own stories, but rather confess them courageously and pray for God's help for us to be transformed into the people we are meant to be. Living well means we take steps to develop our character so that we are not assaulted with hidden sins, secrets that destroy, or behavior that needs to be changed. Strengthening our spiritual lives through the spiritual disciplines of prayer, meditation, and liturgy, through retreats and spiritual readings, through works of art, concern for others, acts of mercy, keeping our affairs in order, and in general taking full responsibility for our lives means we have a far better chance of arriving at the threshold of death with a reasonably clean slate. Then there is no ammunition for the demons of our minds, our souls, or other realms of creation to attack us. Then we are not accused of infidelities and betrayals, of severe neglect or of violence. By this time, our most serious flaws have been dealt with, and we have become more and more whole and Christlike. That is our calling as Christians.

Over the three-hundred-year period during which the handbooks flourished, the art of holy dying came to include the art of holy living. One holy path could not exist without the other. If we want to die well, it is advisable to avoid living as if there is no tomorrow, leaving our practical affairs untended, and being unaccountable for the harm we cause others by our actions.

Despair can also be the result of a sudden and severe encounter with reality. Seeing ourselves as we really are, and not according to the facades we have erected for self-preservation and camouflage, can be devastating. Deep denial about ourselves can often cause a breakdown. Nevertheless, there is always hope. A breakdown can be the first sign of a spiritual break*through*. It is never too late to call on the mercy of God. It is never too late to begin the healing and transformation process. That is the great and astounding wonder of our God.

WOODCUT 2B

HOPE

"WITH THE ANGEL who is consoling Moriens with the words 'Nequaquam desperes' are the saints who have best known the mercy of God—St. Mary Magdalene (shown here in the older understanding as being the same woman as the biblical woman who anointed Jesus' feet with her spikenard of precious ointment); St. Peter with the cock that was the symbol of his fall and the key that showed how completely he was forgiven; Dismas, the good thief tied to his cross; St. Paul hurled from his horse on the road to Damascus. One devil is retreating under the bed; the other says, 'Victoria michi nulla.'"[2] The mercy in this picture is palpable. When one is overcome with despair of any worth to God or others, there comes before the failing heart of Moriens a parade of mercy, a procession of great saints who sinned greatly before coming to know the forgiveness and everlasting mercy of God in Christ. These same saints may inspire us today in our times of despair.

Remedy: Hope

"O afflicted one, storm-tossed, and not comforted,
  I am about to set your stones in antimony,
  and lay your foundations with sapphires.
I will make your pinnacles of rubies,
  your gates of jewels,
  and all your wall of precious stones.
All your children shall be taught by the LORD,
  and great shall be the prosperity of your children.
In righteousness you shall be established;
  you shall be far from oppression, for you shall not fear;
  and from terror, for it shall not come near you."

ISAIAH 54:11–14 (FROM THE EASTER VIGIL)

* * *

The healing balm for the spiritual crisis of despair is found once again in prayer and in narrative. This is the pattern of the *Ars Moriendi*. The remedies are simple. Perhaps deceptively simple, as they require discipline. The remedies are spiritually rigorous and demanding: Pray. Pray without ceasing (1 Thessalonians 5:17). Gather together and pray. Pray alone, and pray with others. Tell your stories, and retell the stories of the saints and holy men and women of history. Sing to the Lord. For in Word and prayer, storytelling and song, we find assurance that God is always ready to forgive. The delay has been our own. Despite the simplicity, prayer is often the hardest habit to form in our busy lives. Bad habits come easy, and the bondage they cause does not surrender readily. Good habits, on the other hand, take real work to form, but they not only form, they in turn form us. And they have the power to endure onslaughts such as a crisis of despair.

At some point, when we face our own death, we are likely to hope there are those around us who have the habit of prayer. If we have been people of prayer ourselves, we will know how important and how effective it is, and we will desire the beauty, strength, and grace of being surrounded by such firm bonds of love and faith. If we have not been people of prayer, we may find ourselves in the "foxhole" position—beginning to pray only when a crisis strikes, an allusion to soldiers who became prayerful when they found themselves in the trenches of battle, praying to live, praying to make it out alive. We do the same thing. We are diagnosed with cancer, for example, and we pray furiously, perhaps for the first time in years. We might then very much want to find some friends or spiritual guides who are well acquainted with prayer. We may then find comfort in the prayers of others and hope to learn to pray and amend our lives ourselves.

The alternative to the foxhole prayer, if we have learned to pray in good times, is that we turn to prayer as the only way we know to really live and the only way to embrace the frightening diagnosis of an illness. In this case, prayer is the natural response, rather than the last-ditch effort to bargain with a Creator we have ignored until this crisis came along. It is the better of the two situations, to find oneself already conversant with prayer when the crisis occurs.

Sometimes the problem is with what we think prayer is. And with what we don't think it is. The monastics have always known that prayer means not only gathering together but also carrying prayer into the work of the day, the meals of the day, the relationships of the day. We hear it in this portion of the ancient prayer attributed to Saint Patrick, called the Breastplate of Saint Patrick:

Christ behind and before me, Christ beneath and above me,
Christ with me and in me, Christ around and about me,
Christ on my left and on my right, Christ when I rise in the morning,
Christ when I lie down at night, Christ in each heart that thinks of me,
Christ in each mouth that speaks of me, Christ in each eye that sees me,
Christ in each ear that hears me.

We do not have to be monks or contemplative religious women or men to learn from the ancient wisdom and attention to prayer that is part of our spiritual heritage. We can give ourselves to the person in a spiritual crisis, while still taking care of ourselves and our other responsibilities. We can find ways to share the time. We need to share the spiritual care of one another so that no one is overburdened and becomes ill themselves, or resentful of the burden. This is an ideal worth striving for, where no one person is expected to give more caregiving than they can manage and remain healthy themselves.

We can create liturgies to pray with the sick and share the crisis, or form gathering times to pray at the home or the hospital bed of a sick person. We can translate these same ideas into praying with and for those who are suffering despair caused by fear, doubt, anxiety, loneliness, and major catastrophes such as divorce, death of a loved one, or the loss of a job or career. Prayer is the key in each instance. We cannot overstate the case for prayer.

Our medieval predecessors included particular saints in their handbooks for dying well, so that everyone could learn which saints had stories to tell and whom to pray intercessions to in a particular crisis. For the crisis of despair, we see an array of sinners who were forgiven much and brought to sainthood depicted in these picture books of holy dying. These books were known as "xylographic" editions, and in them we see Saint Mary

Magdalene, from whom seven devils were cast and who went on to become the Apostle to the apostles; Saint Peter, whose fervor for Jesus was matched by his spectacular betrayal at the time of Jesus' own crisis, but who goes on not only to sainthood but to be the rock upon which Jesus built his church; Saint Paul is shown being thrown from his horse on the road to Damascus—the chief persecutor of Christians who became the architect of the Church; and Saint Dismas, the good thief, who hung on the cross next to Jesus and was welcomed into paradise that very same day. The mercy in these pictures is palpable. When one is overcome with despair, when it's impossible to believe that one is of any worth to God or to others, along comes the procession of great saints who were first—the greatest of sinners. These beloved ones of God knew all too well the forgiveness and everlasting mercy of God in Christ. These same saints inspire us today from the canon of Scripture and from the tradition of the Church.

The additional remedy introduced in this crisis is the need for a method of confession. For the *Ars Moriendi*, and for Catholic Christians today, this brings us again to our wealth of sacrament, our healing ritual of confession. For it is unconfessed sin that torments the dying person. It is unresolved and unamended actions that haunt and produce wells of guilt from which we, like Moriens, draw and drink despair. In the tradition of holy dying, the despairing one is reminded that nothing can separate us from the love of God if we receive the mercy that is offered. Even deathbed repentance is accepted by our loving God. Saint Paul tells us in Romans that "there is therefore now no condemnation for those who are in Christ Jesus" (8:1). He also tells us nothing will separate us from the love of God: "For I am convinced that neither death, nor life, nor angels, nor rulers, nor things present, nor things to come, nor powers, nor height, nor depth, nor anything else in all creation, will be able to separate us from the love of God in Christ Jesus our Lord" (Romans 8: 38–39). Jesus told the parable of the vineyard, where even the latecomers received the full benefit of their master's wealth of mercy and generosity.[3]

Though it is not advisable to wait until one is on one's deathbed to decide to seek the mercy of God, nevertheless, the only sin that will thwart us in this crisis is the sin of despairing of God's forgiveness. To despair of God's mercy is an affront to a loving God. The Good News continues to be preached, even unto the deathbed.

For those who concern themselves with how a dying person may receive and "do" penance, God's mercy is larger and more compassionate than our need to perform a work. The sickness is part of the pastoral care and understanding, and God is not unaware of our condition. Further, it is important for those whose sense of God is that of a punitive parent seeking to inflict punishment to learn a new understanding of God and of the concept of penance. For God is the God of prodigals and prostitutes, as well as the God of prophets and saints. Reconciliation, the key to moving out of despair, is medicine, not punishment. It is the prescription for the soul. It corrects and rehabilitates us. Sometimes medicine is difficult to take, such as making amends might be, but for healing to take place, it is essential.

In the sacramental confession of penance and reconciliation, a wise and pastorally sensitive priest will apply medicine, not punishment. In the crisis, prayer suffices. Contrition suffices. And if you have a gifted and generous and creative confessor, you may find your "penance" to be a gift as well, surprising you with its mercy, its life-giving properties, and its reflection of the love of Christ.

Meditation

(A GUIDED MEDITATION ON THE PRAYER OF SAINT FRANCIS)

This meditation may be prayed as a multi-voice piece, within a liturgy, or it may simply be used for solo reading and meditation.

For Liturgical Use: Instrumental music beneath verses, followed by a moment of silent meditation after each response by the assembly or small prayer group: "Lord make me an instrument of your peace." Music resumes with each spoken verse. Pause for silence at the end of each verse.

(Assembly Response: R/: Lord, make me an instrument of your peace.)

V1: *Lord, make me an instrument of your peace.*

Draw near to us, O God, that we may hear the rhythm of peace as a heartbeat. Create calm from the storm of our anxiety; create clarity from the shadows of our doubt; create cool winds from the heat of our anger. Shape us as clay soft to your touch, and be our sure surprise—channeling peace through our lives that may flow bountifully outward to others.

Maker of peace, hear our prayer and light our path.

R/: Lord, make me an instrument of your peace.

(Silence)

V2: *Where there is hatred let me sow love.*

Still the shallow breathing of hatred, O God, that we may take in the breath of love and live in your presence. Quiet our discord and soothe our minds; quiet our speech and sooth our burning tongues; quiet our despair and soothe our emotions. Scatter seeds of love on holy ground, and make of us a fertile people. Wash clean our hearts that we may pour out love like rain on dry and empty places.

Maker of peace, hear our prayer and light our path.

R/: *Lord, make me an instrument of your peace.*

(*Silence*)

V1: *Where there is injury let me sow pardon.*

Bind our wounds, O God, that we may heal the wounds of others. Anoint us with your holy oil and heal our brokenness; anoint our words and fill them with harmony; anoint our waking hours and be present in all we say and do. As a balm to a wound, let our words reconcile what is torn and battered.

Maker of peace, hear our prayer and light our path.

R/: *Lord, make me an instrument of your peace.*

(*Silence*)

V2: *Where there is doubt, faith.*

Touch our lack of faith with the hands that bore the cross, that Christ who is our light may shine through our darkest hours. Light our path with Brother Sun and Sister Moon; light our minds with the dawn of salvation; light our prayers with the fragrant incense of love. Be our bright shadow on moonless nights and our sight through mist and rain.

Maker of peace, hear our prayer and light our path.

R/: Lord, make me an instrument of your peace.

(*Silence*)

V1: *Where there is despair, hope.*

Hear our cry in times of desperation, O God, that our voices may give way to new hope. Grant to us the anticipation of new life; grant to us anticipation of a harvest of hope; grant to us anticipation of a horizon beyond despair. Shield us from all evil, that we may find strength and share our sure hope with others.

Maker of peace, hear our prayer and light our path.

R/: Lord, make me an instrument of your peace.

(*Silence*)

V2: *Where there is darkness, light.*

Dispel the gloom of dark nights, O God, that we may rise with Christ and bear witness to your resurrection. Greet our darkest sins with forgiveness; greet our failure to love with new chances and new days; greet our hardened hearts with the gentle light of hope. Engulf us in your risen light that we may shine as your children in this world.

Maker of peace, hear our prayer and light our path.

R/: Lord, make me an instrument of your peace.

(*Silence*)

V1: *And where there is sadness, joy.*

Carry our tears in holy vessels for us, O God, that they may be used to moisten the ground of our compassion. Hold our sadness in safekeeping; hold our trembling hands with firm support; hold our grief in tabernacles of love. Keep our sadness as relics of healing power, that these broken pieces of life may be touched upon to heal others and bring them joy.

Maker of peace, hear our prayer and light our path.

R/: Lord, make me an instrument of your peace.

(*Silence*)

V2: *O Divine Master, grant that I may not seek so much to be consoled as to console.*

Favor us with consolation, O God, that we may walk as people of consolation; favor us with comfort, that we may speak as people of consolation; favor us with solace, that we may listen as people of solace; favor us with wisdom, that we may see your face in the eyes of others each day of our lives. Only that we may give away these gifts, do we ask these favors in your name.

Maker of peace, hear our prayer and light our path.

R/: Lord, make me an instrument of your peace.

(Silence)

V1: *To be understood as to understand, to be loved as to love.*

Free us from the bondage of self, O God, that we may do your will. See within the movements of our hearts; see within the secrets we labor to conceal; see within the whirlwind of our souls. With your divine eye you love us as we are, and as we will be. Free us from all that holds back our love, that we may love you above all, and love one another as you have loved us.

Maker of peace, hear our prayer and light our path.

R/: *Lord, make me an instrument of your peace.*

(Silence)

V2: *For it is in giving that we receive.*

Teach us to give, that we may echo your generous love in all we say and do. Show us the way to give our time wisely; show us the way to give our resources to those in need; show us the way to become teachers of love. Grant us open minds and hearts to receive all your treasures that the Kingdom of God may be seen in the hearts of your people.

Maker of peace, hear our prayer and light our path.

R/: *Lord, make me an instrument of your peace.*

(Silence)

VI: *It is in forgiving that we are forgiven,*
    and it is in dying that we are born to eternal life –

And so *we stand* and pray, together with Saint Francis and all the saints before us, in the words that Jesus taught us: Our Father...

Amen.

May the Peace of Christ be with you always.

(Closing song, if used liturgically)

Prayer

From the Litany of Confession

"According to the multitude of your mercies,
cleanse my iniquity,"
O Star-like sun,
O guiding light,
O home of the planets,
O fiery-maned and marvelous One,
O fertile, undulating, fiery sea,
Forgive.
O fiery glow,
O fiery flame of Judgment,
Forgive.
O holy story-teller, holy scholar,
O full of holy grace, of holy strength,
O overflowing, loving, silent One,
O generous and thunderous giver of gifts,
Forgive.
O rock-like warrior of a hundred hosts,
O fair crowned One, victorious, skilled in battle,
Forgive.[4]

·III·

The Third
Spiritual Crisis
and Remedy

WOODCUT 3A

IMPATIENCE

"ONLY ONE DEVIL is tempting Moriens in this picture, but he is succeeding very well; and his 'Quam bene decepi eum' suggests that he realizes his success. Moriens, having overturned the bedside table and with it a bowl, a glass, and a spoon, is now kicking the doctor, who is retreating in alarm. The wife of the sick man extends her hand to him compassionately and says, 'Ecce quantum penam patitur.' In the foreground stands a maid holding in one hand a glass and in the other a plate upon which is the leg of a fowl."[1] This is a picture to which many who have ministered to a sick person, or those who have suffered any prolonged illness, can attest. The temptation by the sick person to attack the doctor and any and all caregivers is quite common.

Crisis: Impatience

And we want each one of you to show the same diligence,
so as to realize the full assurance of hope to the very end,
so that you may not become sluggish,
but imitators of those who through faith and patience
inherit the promises.

HEBREWS 6:11–12

．　．　．

In the year 2000, while the world was swaying with millennium fever and the Jubilee doors of the Church creaked open for a season of recognizing our indulgent God of mercy, I became radically impatient. Less than indulgent. Nothing was as it should be, and I was well beyond any patient endurance of my plight. Work, love, money, security, parenting—nothing was right with my world. It was while I was spiraling into a black hole of no return that some very wise friends noticed something was more than a little amiss with me. These perceptive and loving people suggested that I see a doctor who specializes in—dare I say it?—depression. My friends were convinced I was severely depressed and told me that depression was one thing from which I did not need to continue to suffer. There was help, they explained.

I never knew I was depressed because I had lived all my life with a chronic type of depression. And as I related in the first spiritual crisis, I had medicated my depression with steady treatments of wine each night. Thus, it was only in peeling away the layers of the onion, the metaphor that is so often used by those in recovery, that I was free to receive the truth, the gift of depression, and the gift of its treatment. Only by first dealing with the crisis bound up in addiction was I free to be healed of the biological illness. It was a shock, though, that after over a year of sobriety I found myself feeling worse than ever, unmedicated, with the raw experience of clinical depression bearing down on my whole being.

There was a clear family history of the illness, but I could see this only after my own first crisis was met. The family curse, as one sibling put it, was untreated in the others. As far as my own emotions and thoughts, the cloud of depression had colored everything, all my life. It was all I ever knew. I was highly functioning. I continued to work and to have successes, big successes in my life, but the mystery of my pain remained unfathomable to me. By the time my friends shared their concerns, I was ready to hear them. And when I eventually went to see a "physician of the mind," I was in despair. I was losing faith. The crises were mounting. Though I was willing to get help, I was impatient with everyone, mere mortals that they were, and I often convinced myself that the only solution to my despair and loss of faith was a final solution. I fantasized about committing suicide. How would I do it? Where would I do it? What about my son? My son had anchored me in reality for years, but now he too was growing up and before long, he would be on his own. Then I was free to choose death, I thought, because who can live with this pain. I was sober. I had no intention of resorting to drinking again. So in the bizarre twists of the mind that accompany depression, I thought, "If I can't drink, then I'm just going to have to end my life." It made sense in the grip of the moment, in the abyss of what seemed to be a land of no return. It must be very difficult for the average person to understand the level of emotional pain and torment that can lead someone to consider death as a solution. But it is very real to those who have experienced this particular dark night of the soul. I had hit bottom and was ready to give up the depressive state, a state I had hidden so well from most who knew me, and ready to surrender my illness to God to seek healing.

I believed in God, always. But I didn't want to believe in those increasingly common occurrences of suicidal fantasies. I couldn't even get out of bed toward the end of this period, and I had never plunged to that depth before. Still, no one really knew, since I was working out of my home office at the time, just how bad things were. They didn't know until I finally started talking, and fear of death more than desire for it caused me to speak up in bewilderment. God was with me, that was clear, as soon as I asked for help.

I had so much faith, or so I thought, but my experience was belying that faith and making it seem more like naiveté. There was no rationale to the dark spiral into which I had plunged by the time my friends gently insisted I get some help. I still did not know, that is *really* know, that I was depressed. As ludicrous as that may sound, for someone who has suffered any kind of chronic pain or illness, there is no real basis for comparison. Doesn't everybody feel this way? How could I have known, if that perpetual sadness was something I always lived with, and if the degrees of despair and sadness were all that varied over the years? This was a kind of living death. And like the dying person portrayed in the early visual versions of the *Ars Moriendi* in the third spiritual crisis, I was the sick one who was lashing out at those who cared for me. In the woodcuts we see our friend Moriens suffering mightily at this midpoint in the spiritual crises of dying. In the scene, only one demon works his ill will upon the patient. But it is succeeding very well, for Moriens is shown kicking the doctor who is trying to administer medicine, railing at his wife who is merely trying to comfort him, and knocking over the beside table that contains medication and nourishment. Others in the room are also on the receiving end of his barrage of anger, profanity, and seeming ingratitude.

Now, anyone who has been around someone dealing with a prolonged sickness can attest to such a scene. Or those who have been sick will recognize it themselves, maybe sheepishly. I also recognize it in my own battle with depression. And then, when treatment is finally offered, we want all to be well and well quickly! I certainly did.

We live in a culture that does not value patience. We see it in the "crisis of civility" that journalists are now bemoaning in the daily papers and the daily broadcast news. There are all kinds of names for it, but most include the word "rage." There is road rage and air rage and supermarket rage and student rage and even church rage when the behavior and the "right to rage" leak into our society like arsenic-laced water.

When a woman is diagnosed with breast cancer, impatience overwhelms her. When a man has triple bypass surgery and cannot just return to life as he has known it, impatience once again rears its head. Caregivers feel the barbs, spouses take the heat, and we find that there is far more to recovery from illness than simply making it through the surgery or the initial treatment. It often involves a complete reworking of our lifestyle, and that can affect the entire family. Everyone wants things to be as they were, before the crisis.

If the crisis is a job loss, impatience lurks behind the weeks that may extend to months before one secures a desirable position. We may lash out in the grim reality of unemployment, the financial stress, or the umpteenth rejection letter.

If divorce has shaken our lives, we may feel impatience about our new lives as single persons, as single parents, unable to free ourselves from sadness and loneliness. We don't want to date, and when we do, things don't turn out as planned. We aren't ready for a new relationship, or we move too quickly to be in one. We are impatient for life to be where we want it to be, and that crisis is likely to affect others who love us, or who would just like to be our friends. We have to meet this crisis somehow, some way, and emerge from it better people, or we will die in anguish and cast a pall of mean-spiritedness over others as well. If we get stuck in the crisis, it will color the rest of our lives.

When I began my combination treatment of therapy and medication for depression I had learned something along the way: the need to be patient with myself and patient with the treatment. I wasn't going to feel better right away. It would take time. It would take work. It would take *patience*.

Doctors point out that patients often give up on treatment before it has a chance to work. They want immediate results. This is true whether we are talking about a round of antibiotics or a lifetime regimen of medicine. Patients simply don't want to wait. Or, they stop taking the medication too soon, setting themselves up for relapses. They don't want to wait until the side effects eventually dissipate. They insist on something quicker, which in their minds equals "better." Perhaps no one knows better the level of frustration, knows what it feels like to be "kicked by the impatient patient," than health-care professionals.

I learned to wait it out, and the gift of patience has been the most precious gift I have ever received. The change in my health is truly remarkable. I continue to get better. The cloud I lived under is gone. I am able to see without a veil before my eyes day and night. Sometimes a veil is a handy thing to have, as we shall see as we continue our pilgrimage through the spiritual crises and remedies. But everything has its season. When God chooses to heal and give us new life, then it is not the time for veils. Then it is time to share with others our own stories in hopes of offering solace, courage, and comfort. I did not get well alone. I was ready to receive healing only because others walked with me, told me their stories, and prayed with me. That is the essence of holy living, holy dying, and the holiness of healing. Healing is a sacred art. To receive healing for impatience we will need to walk with our own sacredness—with our bodies as the temple of the

Holy Spirit and our minds as the seat of our soul. We will need to break away from the culture of instant gratification and instant "feel-good" opportunities. We will need to detach from those who, however well meaning, may sabotage our efforts with negativity or false hopes. We may need to embrace the suggestions of people we may have pooh-poohed when we weren't ready to hear the truth, such as when we deny the services of a doctor until the symptoms threaten to overwhelm us. Everything changes in a crisis. The world goes topsy-turvy. But that can sometimes be the best thing that can happen. Let us now turn ourselves over to the remedy for impatience, as we continue on our pilgrimage of holy living and holy dying.

WOODCUT 3B

PATIENCE

"MORIENS HAS OVERCOME impatience, inspired by the angel and by those holy
ones who have suffered most—St. Stephen in the habit of a monk, with his stones
in his scapular; St. Barbara with her tower; St. Katherine of Alexandria with her wheel;
St. Lawrence with the gridiron on which he was roasted; and especially Our Lord, with head
thorn-crowned and in His hands the scourges. Beside Him stands the Eternal Father. One
devil disappears under his bed, saying, 'Sum captivatus'; another, crushed by defeat, says,
'Labores amisi.' In this picture, as in no other except the last, the hands of Moriens are
clasped in prayer."[2] Like those who have been forgiven the most in the remedy for despair,
the communion of saints surrounds Moriens accompanied by a choir of those who have
overcome the worst stages of death.

Remedy:
Patience

Better is the end of a thing than its beginning.
ECCLESIASTES 7:8

. . .

In *The Art of Holy Dying* impatience was often compared to purgatory: the endurance needed to gain patience was a process of purging the spirit. It was a type of purification, or cleansing. The rationale was that if endurance produced patience and patience qualified as an integral part of the purification process, then this was a desirable and profitable quality to cultivate. Any purgation of our souls that could be achieved in this life meant less and less time spent in the purifying process of purgatory, after death. The image of fire was used to envision purgatory, but not the fire of damnation. Rather it is the artisan's fire that purifies gold, that sheds the dross and produces precious metal. So it was for humanity. Purgatory would shed our human dross, and leave us refined gold for our God. In medieval times, and even to some extent still lingering in the religious imagination today, is the idea of negotiating for time off in purgatory based on our good behavior in this life.

Even without such negotiating tactics in mind, though, patience does indeed purge the spirit. It does have the effect of washing us as purifying water or, if you prefer, a fire of purification. But it is an extremely difficult thing to genuinely experience.

Our help in times of spiritual peril is yet again in communal form. This is what our predecessors knew instinctively. Our North American culture of self-sufficiency in all things—or its alter ego, co-dependency in all things—produces people who have no conception of either the need for community in the care of the sick and dying or the unhealthy lack of boundaries that can develop between the sick and their caretakers. For example, a son or daughter becomes the designated caregiver for the sick and elderly mother. The demands of this role may be so great that the adult child is overwhelmed and neglects his or her own family, work, and personal needs for a balanced life. If the caregiver believes that only he or she can provide the proper care, and the mother becomes so completely dependent on the son or daughter that she inflicts guilt at the mere suggestion of shared caregiving, then a co-dependent relationship that is extremely unhealthy for both mother and adult child exists. In the communal model, however idealized this may be, there would be shared caregiving, whether among family members, friends, or even professional health-care workers, if that is necessary to give everyone adequate time to take care of themselves and be present to their spouses and their own children and friends. It is up to the healthy to be clear about their own needs and to set limits as to how much they can reasonably expect to give. Otherwise, the caregivers will become sick themselves, physically or emotionally or both, and far too depleted to continue to give to the patient.

At the same time, the fact that many people lie alone in hospital rooms hidden from view while sanitized images of all-pervasive toned and youthful bodies permeate popular culture is tragic. In our daily quests to deny death, we watch news of violence and terror through distant eyes that show us only what we want to see: that death on television, or death as entertainment in the movies, is not the same as in real life. We avoid it, hoping it will never touch us. But all too often it does touch us, or someone in our family, or someone down the street from us, and we are left without the coping skills or the faith to withstand the assault.

Some cultures find the very idea of leaving someone alone in a hospital room to be inconceivable. In Hispanic culture, for example, no one is left alone during sickness, especially a loved one. But the practice of isolating the sick is the norm in our society, which is ironic given the medical advances and technological wonders. In some ways, particularly in our relationship with mortality, we are in need of remedial learning. When I advocate the retrieval of a tradition from late medieval and Renaissance times, I am advocating foremost for the return of a community of faith that is involved in how its members die. I am urging that we bring back into our churches and into our spiritual practices communal prayer and the art of companioning and living well and dying well.

Sacramentally and liturgically, this community involvement consists of full, active, and conscious participation for all in the Church, from birth to death. We have already addressed this interwoven nature of our lives from baptism to funeral rite. But before the funeral, before the burial, our participation is our collective vocation. Liturgies of lamentation are crucial for those who live with life-threatening illness, or those who have lost a child, or those who are divorced, recovering from addiction, or who have otherwise stared into the reality of death or deep loss. We can pray and weep and sing and find peace and joy in the midst of trials and the mystery of suffering. We need not, and should not, go it alone.

I had the opportunity to craft "A Day for Those Who Have Lost a Child" for my local church, which also happens to be a shrine and place of pilgrimage. The death of a child is a loss of incomparable grief, whether that child is an infant, a youngster, a teenager, or a grown son or daughter. It seems totally unnatural for a child to die before one's parents. During this day we presented support in the form of speakers and counselors, artists and parents who bore witness to the tragedy. We also presented a liturgy of lamentation, a place of sacred and safe space to come before God and lament the injustice, the pain, the broken dreams, and the harshest of realities. Parents came in procession with candles for their deceased babies and grown children. Tears flowed together with praise, as prayer lifted the spirit. They wept and yet were thankful, groaned and yet were grateful, somehow, for faith and for the hope in Christ that carried them through their journey. Here was an example of the power of community to open its arms in solidarity and to receive those in the body of Christ who suffer and mourn, to stand with them and pray with them in remembrance of lost lives.

In this there was also remembrance of how often it is that children somehow manage to teach us how to die. For seldom does the child seem to meet illness, suffering, and death with the same level of bitterness and despair we create as adults. Somehow, in their innocence, children teach us to live as if every breath of life is vital and conscious, and to die with love and grace and dignity. We can accompany the children, but they accompany our adult grief in ways we could never imagine. These children are truly a gift of precious life. They are our teachers in death.

• • •

To achieve a community where burdens of suffering and death are shared means to create a community that embraces catechesis to learn the art of living well and dying well. It means pastoral sensitivity is a priority for priests and other members of pastoral teams, both lay and ordained, and it means consciously creating an environment where those who are sick or suffering other types of loss are joined by a community of faith who accompany them on their journey. It means a catechesis of living well, so that *all* learn by practicing the art of living well how to approach their own death with peace.

How can we learn this? Through setting aside time for spiritually oriented adult programs where these practices are introduced and encouraged, and where an ongoing network of support can be nurtured. Speakers can be brought in for formation days or evenings. They might represent a variety of professions, from healthcare to clergy, from theologians to activists in the area of health and dying. Artists who paint, sculpt, write, photograph, or utilize other mediums for expression can share their art and their inspiration. Musicians can perform soothing music for the sick. Books on the topic can be made available in parish libraries, and groups can form for mutual support. Parish liturgists can work on developing liturgies that go beyond the usual healing masses, and provide liturgies of lamentation, or prayer services for those living with terminal or chronic illness, or reconciliation services for those facing death. Some spiritual directors may be willing to make themselves available to those who seek to find God in the midst of their suffering. Brainstorming is sure to introduce other ideas so that we can learn to live well and to die well, as members each of the body of Christ.

· · ·

Our predecessors called upon saints who showed remarkable patience in their lives. In the woodcut depicting the overcoming of impatience, we see Saint Stephen in the habit of a monk with the stones that were hurled at him held in his scapular; Saint Barbara with her tower, the place where she was held before martyrdom; Saint Katherine of Alexandria with the wheel that was used as an instrument of her death; and Saint Lawrence likewise the implement of his torture, the gridiron. Such depictions were meant to remind the dying person that the martyrs suffered unspeakable horrors with endurance and holiness. The most important depiction of course is that of Jesus Christ himself, his head crowned with thorns, and in his hands, the scourges that were used upon his back. Beside Jesus stands his heavenly Father. The demons flee from these scenes. The faith of the holy ones, and especially the salvation wrought by Christ, is too much for them to bear.

In the depictions, Moriens, the dying Everyman, has his hands clasped in prayer. Prayer, prayer, and more prayer is the remedy for these spiritual crises. Just as we learn to call upon the saints who were forgiven the most as the remedy for despair, so in this crisis we are advised to seek the intercession of those who suffered the most and did so with great courage and steadfast faith. These saints bring with them choirs who sing and surround the dying person. So, too, we call upon the saints for intercessory prayer, and we pray to Christ our salvation and our hope, and seek the legendary patience of these saints. And as in the past, we just may find ourselves surrounded by a communion of saints and choirs of angels unseen, as well as the comfort of our community of faith and our family of loved ones.

Later versions of the art of holy dying, such as Jeremy Taylor's exquisitely written seventeenth-century treatise which represents a post-Reformation Anglican view, cite gratitude as the remedy for impatience. Making gratitude lists when we are unable to see the good around us, and helping one another to write and speak those things for which we are grateful, remains a very effective antidote.

At this station in our pilgrimage through *The Art of Holy Dying*, we enter into a meditation that focuses once again on the Passion of Christ, remembering that the Passion was the heart of healing prayer and meditation for the original works of living well and dying well, and that we need this Passion of Christ no less today than did our ancestors in Christ. In solidarity with Christ's wounds, in hope for his gift of endurance, and in light of his holy perseverance, we pray.

Meditation

(FROM THE SEVEN LAST WORDS OF JESUS)

This meditation may be prayed as a multi-voice piece, within a liturgy, or it may simply be used for solo reading and meditation.

"I Thirst"

Without your drops of living water on our tongues
we shall cease to sing your praise, O God.
Without cups and streams and showers of cooling waters
we shall not live another day.
In drought our spirits search the arid land for a drink
to ease our parched and brittle tongues.
In dry and deserted places we become misshapen by thirst,
twisted by unmet longing,
and unable to quench the thirst of pilgrims passing through.
We hear a distant cry: "I thirst."
He who is Wonderful, Counselor, Prince of Peace—*the Teacher*—
is thirsting on the cross and cries out, like us, for cool waters.
We hear ancient torment as if today,
and his cry is the cry of clarity,
his longing as pure as the water he seeks.
We have plunged and sprinkled,
prayed and sung—
taking vows through moving waters—
to follow this Christ of the Jordan River,
to follow this Wonder-Worker who changed water into wine,
to follow this Prophet of the woman at the well,
to follow this Man who walked on water,

to follow this Healer of the Sea of Galilee,
to follow this Wounded God-Man who hangs on the tree

and cries out, "I thirst!"

We follow, we thirst, we cry out,
and we shake our hands at God-who-let-this-happen!
What God is this whose only Son thirsts
at the hands of mockery, insult, and death?
Whose Son thirsts and turns from bitter offerings
and casts his spirit upon the mercy of thirst itself—and dies?

He dies!

He dies from the thirst of the bloodthirsty,
who sought to silence Love.
He dies of thirst:
thirsting for justice,
thirsting for peace,
thirsting for each one of us whom he loves and longs for,
and he will accept no less than
the cooling, cleansing water of life.

We *watch*, longing ourselves to cool his thirst
and ease the cup of suffering.

We *remember* rituals of water,
where repentance changed our lives
and formed us anew,

clean and pure in purpose and in hope.
We *imagine* rivers of peace where nails and spears and
pieces of cross may be tossed into the path of the sea forever!

We *look again*, and long to wash the feet of he whose
eyes now cloud in pain as he cries,

"I thirst!"

We glimpse the cost of love. Thirst. Crossbearing thirst.
And some flee,
and some few stay,
and stand before the thirst of ages and cry together with
Jesus our Lord,

"I thirst!"
God, grant life-giving waters to those who seek your face,
brave the elements to pray,
and watch and listen with our beloved teacher,
who taught us how to pray.
Grant, O Lord,
Rain for the lowly,
Streams for the pilgrim,
Wells for the sturdy, and
Springs for the children who dance in the light.
Grant peace from suffering to the teacher of peace,
whose righteous thirst beckons us all.

Peace of Christ be with you always,

R/. And also with you.

Prayer
Blessings
(ADAPTED FROM THE TRADITIONAL CELTIC BLESSING)

Be each saint in heaven,
Each sainted woman in heaven,
Each angel in heaven
Stretching their arms for you,
Smoothing the way for you,
When you go this way
Over the river hard to see;
Or when you go that way home,
Over the River hard to see.

May the Father take you
In His fragrant clasp of love,
When you go across the flooding streams
And the black river of death.

The love of our Creator be with you.

Be the eye of God dwelling with you,
The foot of Christ in guidance with you,
The shower of the spirit pouring on you,
Richly and generously.

The love and affection of the heavens be to you,
The love and affection of the saints be to you,
The love and affection of the angels be to you,
The love and affection of the sun be to you,

The love and affection of the moon be to you,
Each day and night of your life,
To keep you from haters,
To keep you from harmers,
To keep you from oppressors.

·IV·

The Fourth
Spiritual Crisis
and Remedy

WOODCUT 4A

SPIRITUAL PRIDE

"FIVE HORRIBLE DEVILS are tempting Moriens to pride in his success against the first three crowns and filling his mind with vainglorious thoughts: 'Gloriare,' they say, and 'Tu es firmus in fide,' 'Coronam meruisti,' 'In paciencia perseverasti,' 'Exaltate ipsum.' In the background stand the Eternal Father, Our Lord, and, in the attitude of prayer, Our Lady, two indistinguishable other saints, and three small children—supposedly a hallucination of the devils to make Moriens believe that he belongs by merit in this holy company."[1] It is notable that the temptation to vainglory, or pride, is not pride in worldly accomplishments, but is here interpreted as spiritual pride, an absence of humility that threatens to jeopardize the real overcoming of temptation.

Crisis:
Spiritual Pride

Pride goes before destruction,
and a haughty spirit before a fall.
PROVERBS 16:18

. . .

I live in Chicago now. I came here in 1997, along with my son, to attend graduate school and study theology, and we have stayed. Since moving from Vermont, we have been living a radically different way of life, from the placid shores of Lake Champlain to the urban, frenetic energy of Lake Michigan. My first impression of Chicago was at night: a glowing, vibrant jewel of a skyline with resplendent architecture that captivated my imagination and my very deep need to see beauty all around me. I thought I had wandered down the yellow brick road and arrived at the Emerald City! I was home. I fell in love with Chicago.

Lately, though, a stubborn problem has developed in "the Loop," the famous center of the city. Windows were popping out of their moorings and crashing to the sidewalks below. Older facades required swift repair. The great architectural beauties needed steady upkeep. Intricate carvings and the stunning gems of the skyline revealed cracks and weaknesses. Mortar, brick, and clay were falling like rain on the busy streets of downtown Chicago. Up went the protective awnings while repairs were on the way, reminding us that sometimes it did indeed seem as if the sky was falling.

All of this was not without tragedy. One of those falling, twirling, cascading windows struck a young mother without warning, immediately taking her life in what could only be described as a freak accident, while her young son screamed in horror and passers-by tried to make sense of it all.

The safety of walking down the street had been deceptive. There was danger, and although some had foreseen this possibility, it was nevertheless a terrible shock and tragedy. More awnings, more precautions, and much reparation are underway in the city of Chicago.

Like walking down the street with a feeling that all is safe, the crisis of spiritual pride can also be deceptive. Spiritual pride is in fact a very tricky crisis of *self*-deception. For this is not pride in accomplishments and life success, rather this pride represents that which comes over the dying person, or the person in a life crisis, when they realize they have successfully overcome the crises of faith, despair, and impatience. It is the pitfall of what was once commonly called "vainglory," which speaks for itself. The glory of spiritual pride is empty. It is vanity. It is all in vain. It is the temptation to believe that we have "arrived" spiritually, and we are now in the clear, above and beyond further spiritual calamities. It is the slippery slope of sliding fast toward the house of mirrors into which the crash and all its accompanying shards of glass is imminent. Those shards can wipe us out in an instant, if we cease to be vigilant over our spiritual well-being. For just when we feel safe, something happens to pierce our sense of security.

The presence of having other people in our life is all the more necessary now, and the assistance of the spiritual director, or soul friend, immeasurably helpful. In the artistic vision of this crisis in the medieval mind, it was imagined that Moriens, our dying friend, was surrounded by God the Father, Christ, Mary, the saints, and three small children.[2] All of this was a deception meant to deceive our friend into thinking that he merited being in the company of these holy ones.

What is missing from Moriens' thinking, or from any of us as we move through life's losses and especially as we get closer to our final pilgrimage of faith toward eternity with Christ, is humility. Humility is not a popular word in our competitive society. The connotation is often associated with weakness, when in fact humility is anything but weakness. It takes a very strong, very secure human being to truly embody humility. The fact that genuine humility is so rarely encountered speaks to the value of its inherent strength. It is a virtue, and those who are virtuous, those who model sacred virtues, are not the most common of human beings. Humility has its roots, as a word, in the earth. A person who is filled with humility is someone who is grounded, steadfast, and centered. If you were in danger, wouldn't you want to be in the presence of someone who was solid, steady, and able to pray for you and draw you toward that center of humility yourself? That is what our *Ars Moriendi* practitioners thought, and that is why they valued the ability to surmount this crisis and become humble.

How shall we differentiate between self-deception and humility today? The litmus test is simple. Humility is the quality of being teachable. A pride-filled person is not teachable. An angry, resentful person is not teachable. A smug, self-righteous person is far from being teachable. And when humility is missing, when that essential quality that enables us to learn and grow and receive the gift of God is missing, we are shortchanged and become sitting ducks for the crash into the house of mirrors described above. Without humility, we career out of control. Hopefully, when faced with the twisted turning mirrors of the funhouse, we see that our reflection was distorted all along. The mirrors of our self-deception and pride only reflect what we want to see, and that only partially. Saint Paul said we see in this life as through a glass darkly, a looking glass, that is: "For now we see in a mirror, dimly, but then we will see face to face. Now I know only in part; then I will know fully, even as I have been fully known" (1 Corinthians 13:12). We stop along the way in our stational liturgy, our pilgrimage with the *Ars Moriendi*, to seek healing for pride and wisdom in how to proceed.

It is possible when locked in this battle for our souls that our spiritual pride will so blind us that we no longer see any need for community, nor the need for prayer, nor any of the very remedies that brought us to this point in the process of facing a major life crisis. We may decide we don't need anything as ritualistic as liturgy, as communal as communion, or as inconvenient as getting up and going to church to give thanks to the God who has brought us thus far. It is a place where the temptation to become arrogant is very great. And indeed we may find ourselves alone again, without community, for who wants to be in the company of arrogance? The spiritual delusion may be very apparent to others while we remain unable to see. We become convinced of our own power to overcome hardship and suffering, and betray all the progress and divine help that has been granted to us up to this point.

I have a childhood friend who refused to go to her own mother's funeral because she thought her own strength was greater and more valuable than any gathering of mourners. She suffered alone. She denied others her valuable presence. Her spiritual arrogance displayed a lack of respect for her mother's spiritual beliefs and made her own arrogance the deciding factor in how she would respond to this very great loss in her life. Her mother had always been there for her, yet she chose not to attend the funeral, even after her mother lost a long battle with cancer. How tragic, and how unnecessary. The one who suffered most in this story was the young woman herself. She sat alone at home with her grief, her arrogance hardening the shell that continued to grow around her in the years to come. For she "didn't believe in" rituals around death, nor did she "believe in" the church of her heritage. What she did "believe in" made her an increasingly shallow person, incapable of being there for others, even in death. She wanted to deny death, to hide it away, to refuse to face it. Like a hospital room in which one is left to die alone with only occasional visitors, this woman sanitized her own experience by refusing to accept the gift of community, the gift of liturgy, the gift of the Eucharist, and the healing voices that could alleviate the pain of death. It doesn't have to be this way. All it takes is a little bit of humility to crack open the door and take one step at a time toward our human frailty, to receive the gift of solace, of lamentation, and of presence given and received.

WOODCUT 4B

HUMILITY

"IN EACH OF THE THREE preceding 'inspiration' pictures there is one angel; here there are three. The most prominent one says, 'Superbos punio,' pointing at hell-mouth, in which three souls are writhing in torture, one a tonsured monk. 'Sis humilis' is upon the scroll borne by another of the angels, and above, in the clouds, the Trinity and Our Lady appear. At the left foot of the bed stands St. Anthony, the hermit, model of humility, with bell and crozier. In the foreground a crouching demon cries, 'Victus sum.'"[3] We are not abandoned. When the temptations become more sophisticated, we are borne up by increasing love and mercy. The antidote to pride is threefold: the Holy Trinity along with three angels, the Virgin Mary, and a hermit-saint enfold the suffering Moriens with consolation and spiritual clarity.

Remedy:
Humility

Lament and mourn and weep. Let your laughter
be turned into mourning and your joy into dejection.
Humble yourselves before the Lord, and he will exalt you.

JAMES 4:9–10

. . .

Turn our joy into dejection? What kind of spiritual care is this for the dying? It is another reality check. Although notoriously practical in his advice, Saint James was not always the most popular scripture writer—we can easily understand why! He had a no-nonsense approach to pastoral care. He simply told it like it was: You've been deceived, so turn to lamentation and cry out to the Lord. If you humble yourselves before God, then and only then, will you realize the exaltation you so desire.

This crisis is so serious that the medieval artisans upped the ante in the pictorial displays. Where before there had been one angel present, now there were three. Souls being drawn into hell are depicted even in the remedy.[4] Those ill-fated souls include the sight of a tonsured monk, sending the message that religious life required more than outward appearances to be sincere and holy. Here also the Holy Trinity appears. Prior to this, there had been God the Father and Christ, but now the entire Trinity is needed to effectively meet this crisis. Mary is present, as she has been, and the saint of the hour is Saint Anthony the hermit, who is the model of humility. The message is clear: We are not abandoned! When the temptations become more sophisticated, we are borne up by increasing love and mercy. The antidote to spiritual pride is threefold: the Holy Trinity, three attending angels, and Mary with Saint Anthony, all of whom enfold the suffering Moriens with consolation, humility, and, finally, spiritual clarity.

Here again, we must not forget the need for prayers and communal support. Our community of faith is obliged to hold up our faith, stand in solidarity with our suffering and dying as members all of the body of Christ. "[W]hereas our more respectable members do not need this. But God has so arranged the body, giving the greater honor to the inferior member, that there may be no dissension within the body, but the members may have the same care for one another. If one member suffers, all suffer together with it; if one member is honored, all rejoice together with it" (1 Corinthians 12:24–26).

Pastoral care that may appropriately come into play at this stage of the spiritual crises of dying warrants particular attention. One of the techniques employed by the *Ars Moriendi* practitioners was commonly known as "the interrogations." The interrogations are essentially scrutinies, or examinations of conscience. We have become familiar with scrutiny rituals in liturgy during the final period of the catechumenate in the Rite of Christian Initiation of Adults, rites that have been retrieved from the ancient church for those seeking initiation as Catholic Christians. These scrutinies occur on the third, fourth, and fifth Sundays of Lent during the eucharistic liturgy. The scrutinies that were part of the *Ars Moriendi* were of a more private nature. In retrieving this practice, which is a combination of spiritual direction and sacramental penance and reconciliation, we also have room for liturgical innovation along the lines of the RCIA scrutinies. We already have communal penance and reconciliation liturgies. The examination of conscience used in those liturgies could be prepared for special groups—those with terminal illnesses, for example. What we have from church history and tradition are sets of questions, or interrogations, that were outlined in the handbooks for the anointing of the sick. What was sought during these intense periods of questioning was a genuine profession of faith. This type of question-and-answer ritual is seen today in some nonsacramental rituals, such as religious professions or lay admission into quasi-religious life. The profession of faith in the *Ars Moriendi* was and is an essential spiritual barometer to assist in determining the state of one's soul at the end of one's life. The interrogations were not the realm of the ordained alone because a shortage of clergy existed at the time these books were written. Therefore, this type of pastoral care could fall to friends and loved ones in the absence of clergy. Of course, the priest was needed for the final sacraments of penance, the anointing of the sick, and the Eucharist.

Today, we can bring the Eucharist to the sick as extraordinary ministers of the Eucharist in times of need or the absence of a priest. We can pray with our loved ones. We can have qualified laypeople lead nonsacramental liturgies of prayer and consolation. And we may, as laypeople, facilitate an examination of conscience for the person who is dying.

The interrogations of the *Ars Moriendi* were deliberately tough, since sincerity of confession was desired, as was authenticity in the profession of faith. We would do well to present this concept, much like tough love, in pastoral care today, within reason and with genuine understanding, wisdom, and compassion. One motivation behind this display of pastoral toughness was the possibility that the dying person might regain health. If that were to happen, then the confessed needed to realize the gravity of any serious sin and be willing to amend their life if God so granted them a return to health. If we recover from a serious illness, if we are cancer survivors, people in recovery, people living with AIDs, if we have a near-death experience and live to tell the tale, then we too should be seeking to amend our lives in any way necessary to live well and holy for the rest of the time God grants us. Our gratitude is all the more real having touched the possibility of death.

In the original handbooks, at the same time that interrogations were present, so too were a series of "obsecrations" for the dying person to pray.

These prayers return the soul to the tender spirit found in the earlier reme-dies for spiritual crises. The Lord is beloved, sweet, and the desire of one's soul. The dying person was also surrounded by "sacramentals," those arti-cles that comfort us as symbols of faith and prayer. Sacramentals included a crucifix, holy water, and other sacred icons. From such a description it is possible to imagine a scene straight out of the movie *The Exorcist.* This would not be so far off the mark as one might think, since the rite of bap-tism and the scrutinies of catechumens contain minor exorcisms, while the sacrament of Penance has long been understood as an exorcistic sacrament. So too are these examinations of conscience for the dying person a form of minor exorcism. An exorcism is, after all, a prayer ritual. Despite the dra-matic displays in movies, it all comes down to prayers for healing; prayers for forgiveness; prayers for restoration to sound health of body, mind, and spirit; and prayers for the dying. These minor exorcisms were and are intended to cleanse and heal our souls and prepare us for whatever God has in store.

Like our predecessors, surrounding ourselves with sacramentals is also a fruitful practice. We are remembered, put back together again spiritually, by the symbols that surround us. For we still revere the crucifix, the symbol of Christ's passion. We still seek to be sprinkled with holy water, and to be reminded of our baptism in the process. We still enjoy the veneration of the saints, and ask for their intercessory prayers on our behalf. Indeed, we still love symbols and sacraments in our lives and in our deaths, as Catholic Christians.

• • •

At this fourth station in our pilgrimage, we turn to a meditation based on the Way of the Cross. In our stational liturgy, from crisis to crisis, we bow to an earlier stational type of prayer, one that is still popular today. Begun by the Franciscans, the stations of the cross provide the backdrop for this original meditation that combines the Way of the Cross with an examination of conscience.

Meditation

This meditation may be prayed as a multi-voice piece, within a liturgy, or it may simply be used for solo reading and meditation.

The Way of the Cross

1. Jesus Is Condemned to Death

Lord, we have sinned in what we have done, and what we have failed to do. In thought and in deed, we have failed to love. You, who though innocent, were condemned in our stead, generously pray for us. When power is abused, when envy consumes us, when we wash our hands of one another and separate ourselves from love, at those times have compassion on us, draw us to yourself, let us stand in the sunlight of your gaze and turn from our sin, that we may be healed. Let our hands be truly clean, save us from our sins, through your cross and resurrection.

We pray to the Lord.

2. Jesus Bears His Cross

Lord, we ask you to keep us faithful in the shadow of the cross. When we have used the gift of speech to mock others, we have done as your persecutors did. Forgive us our sin. When we have misjudged others, we have become as your captors. Forgive us through the gift of the cross. Let the wood you carried be for us a tree of life, springing forth from the announcement of death. Forgive us, and make us whole.

We pray to the Lord.

3. Jesus Falls for the First Time

The road we have traveled has caused us to stumble, to fall, to lose hope that we can ever overcome the sins we struggle with. You suffered as we have suffered. You felt the weight of all of our sins and yet stood again to fulfill the will of the father. Strengthen us when we fall, lift us when we stumble, and raise us to the dignity of daughters and sons of your kingdom. Heal us of our pride as in all humility we ask for your presence to illuminate the dark places of our souls.

We pray to the Lord.

4. Jesus Meets His Mother

Mary, Mother of God, pray for us. Meet us in our despair—in our shame and embarrassment at our sin. When we are ashamed to be seen by those we love, come to us, and in tender mercy intercede for us with Jesus Christ, your son, our Lord and Savior. In love, be present in our hours of confusion. Stand with us at the cross in vigil, waiting in hope for the transforming of our hearts by the gift of Christ's passion.

We pray to the Lord.

5. Jesus Is Helped by Simon

Lord, we have often refused to be helped. We have sinned in our pride and become lost in our own determinations. Yet you who are all power and all love—the Son of God, you who could call angels to your aid—you accepted the help of Simon on the road of suffering. Let *our* self-reliance give way to acceptance of one another on the road to healing. We cannot become whole by struggling alone. We cannot be healed by our own strength. Deliver us from the burden and bondage of self-will. Assist us in our pain and send to us the Simons of our time, who will serve you by lifting the cross with us. Let us become like Simon when we see the suffering of others. Forgive us for our arrogance, and let us receive your gift of love.

We pray to the Lord.

6. *Jesus and Veronica*

We have turned our eyes away and refused to look at suffering. We have presented ourselves as blameless. Shatter our false images, Lord, with an encounter with Calvary. Eye to eye, let us see your face, and soften our hearts through your gaze. In deepest intimacy Veronica reached out for your face, touched your divine presence, and comforted your pain. We ask for this saint's intercession in our own lives, that we might be a people of deep compassion. Imprint your image on the veil of our hearts, that death may not overcome us, that despair will not swallow our spirits, but rather that we will be made whole and blameless by your sacrifice.

We pray to the Lord.

7. *Jesus Falls a Second Time*

We have fallen, and we have caused others to fall. In plots, in actions, in words of ill will—we have made the way difficult for others. Let us fall now before the one who saves us. Let us kneel in our hearts in repentance before the one who in innocence carried our sins to the place where they would have no more power. Jesus, look upon our behavior with forgiveness. We bow before you and ask for your healing mercy. We receive your love in the palms of our open hands. We know you will not turn away from the prayers of your people.

We pray to the Lord.

8. *Jesus Speaks to the Women*

We weep for our sins. In lamentation we look upon your journey of pain, the result of the sins of those you love. Hear our lament. Let our tears cleanse us. Let our tears open us to the mystery of your unending mercy. Let our tears wash one another in rivers of hope. Overturn our sin of self-pity and give us the vision of love.

We pray to the Lord.

9. *Jesus Falls a Third Time*

When trials seem unbearable, when we no longer wish to live, let us fall with you into the arms of the Father—into the care of the One who is mystery and hope. When exhaustion threatens our faith, do not leave us alone in the throes of despair. We are tempted to abandon life itself, to reject the gift hidden in the suffering we endure. Let us fall with you into the only abandonment that gives life—abandonment to your will, to your cross, and to your promise of resurrection. Send your angels to bear us up that we might persevere and catch the embrace of hope.

We pray to the Lord.

10. *Jesus Is Stripped of His Garments*

We have sinned in our words and deeds. We have stripped others of dignity with gossip. We have torn the reputations of others with malice. We are no different than those who sold your garments for profit and mocked you in your nakedness. Heal us.

Strip us of all unworthy speech. Rend our false clothing and let us come before you without the cover of image, without the things that prop our status and hide our true selves. In this moment, in this station of utter humility, we seek to stand in honesty, to stand in vulnerability, and to stand in trust before you. Cover us with robes of forgiveness. Blanket us in the warmth of divine love. Clothe us in new garments of bright transformation.

We pray to the Lord.

11. *Jesus Is Nailed to the Cross*

Your wounds call us to repentance. Spikes driven through your flesh break open for us a new and holy way to live. Lead us as pilgrims of faith, through the suffering sin has caused us to the healing promised by your cross. You have opened

99

the way for us. You have borne all our sin, all our evil, all the ways in which we have fallen short of love. Draw us into the paschal mystery and renew us by the power of forgiveness—the same forgiveness you showed to Saint Dismas, the repentant thief, who upon seeing you and death, saw his salvation and his eternal life. Be our life and our salvation.

We pray to the Lord.

12. *Jesus Dies on the Cross*
We are face to face with death. In dying you transformed death. Take our sins to that place where they are remembered no more. Saint Francis of Assisi said, "It is you who have crucified Jesus, and crucify him still, when you delight in your vices and sins."

We ask for our only delight to be in living in your will for us. Delight in love, delight in hope, delight in the transforming encounter with the shadow of the cross this day. Turn our mourning before the cross into dancing before the empty tomb. We dance in the light: we have this hope, we have this promise.

We pray to the Lord.

13. *Jesus Is Taken Down from the Cross*
Lord, your body is our sacrament of reconciliation. The blood that covered your body has become the wine of new life. Our sins have brought us to death. We confront our sins, we see what we have done, and we ask your forgiveness and mercy. Do not delay in healing our spirits, that we might celebrate your sacrament in this season with newness of life, conversion of heart, and garments of prayer drawn around us.

We pray to the Lord.

14. *Jesus Is Laid in the Tomb*

Let us enter the tomb and lay to rest all that brings death to our spirit. We bury malice and envy. We bury thievery and deception. We bury adultery and the use of others for our own desires. We bury greed, arrogance, and pride. We bury gossip, slander, and ill will. On these and all the sins of our hearts, we plant the stone of burial.

We turn to you, Lord, and ask you to roll away the stones that hold our hearts, our minds, and our spirits in bondage. Open us up to the freedom of repentance. Let us see with clarity. Let us hear the crystalline sound of love. Let us speak in words of praise to you and mercy to others.

As we prepare ourselves to confess our sins, anoint us with your oil of salvation. We humbly ask this in the name of Jesus Christ, who lived and died that we might be one with you, in the power of the Holy Spirit. You are one God, forever, and ever.

Amen.

Prayer

In thin places,
where the dividing line between you and me melts,
where the world between worlds is sighted,
where earth and eternity kiss,
where ancient words are heard and held dear,
and where new voices sound through the veil,
in that place,
on the holy ground,
touch us, O God of tears and prostrate longings,
cause us to know humility.

In thin places,
in between life and death,
in between pride and the fall,
in between forgiveness and refusal,
reach into our hearts,
you have our permission,
and soften the hardened clay with
living waters from your weeping eyes.

In thin places where we see the horizon
of life and death and in-between
hold us hard,
hold us long,
and hold us while humility works its way

into our being and courses through
our veins,
that we might live forever in you,
with Mary, and all the saints before us,
through Christ our beloved Savior and Lord,

Amen.

·V·

The Fifth
Spiritual Crisis
and Remedy

WOODCUT 5A

GREED

"ONE DEMON POINTS to the wife, the children, and the friends of Moriens, standing at the right of his bed ('Provideas amicis'); two others to his possessions—his house with its well-stocked wine cellar and his horse, being led by the groom into the stable ('Intend thesauro'). In some of the xylographic editions (picture books), notably the *editio princeps*, a servant is making more poignant the sick man's concern over his goods by stealing wine from one of the casks."[1] The necessity of letting go of worldly concerns, relationships, and property and focusing on the Passion of Christ, as the *Ars Moriendi* directs, is first met with fierce resistance.

Crisis:
Greed

Jesus looked at him and said, "How hard it is
for those who have wealth to enter the kingdom of God!
Indeed, it is easier for a camel to go through
the eye of a needle than for someone who is rich
to enter the kingdom of God."

LUKE 18:24–25

. . .

It is with fierce resistance that we come to the fifth spiritual crisis, that of greed or avarice. Ask anyone who has had to simplify his or her life unwillingly. It is the crisis of hanging on to possessions, people, places, and ideas. It is the call to engage in the practice of letting go. It is the crisis of clinging to the past, the forceful nostalgia for what has ended and the resistance to change.

There is a contemporary movement that embraces "voluntary simplicity." It is a counter-cultural lifestyle that claims resistance to the relentless acquisition of possessions and money. It sounds wholesome. We should be careful, however, not to be deceived. The simplicity is often far from the ideal once set forth by Henry David Thoreau and Walden Pond. All too often it is a mask for alternative greed, alternative possessiveness, and alternative acquisition. That is how good ideas get twisted. It happens because we are human, and that is the human condition. Much as it is easy to look at ostentatious displays of wealth and point at the speck in our brother or sister's eye, we might want to look at the beam of self-righteousness that can accompany movements of simplicity and asceticism that are well intentioned,

107

but also not without fault. Ask a devout follower of simplicity to give up their solar-powered home and electric car and see what happens. Ask devotees of New England's *Tightwad Gazette* to reconsider their obsessive stinginess or pennywise-pound foolish thinking and see how far you get. Ask someone living "off the grid" in Idaho to relinquish their cabin, their firearms, or their garden, and beware of the outcome.

When the obsessive coupon-clipping mother is asked to toss her file full of coupons for products she would not otherwise purchase, we see a manifestation of greed. When a church leader refuses to turn on the heat blower in the sacristy causing the preparation room to feel more like a freezer than a sacred space—and one that endangers health—we are witnessing the flip side of greed. But we all work through the same human condition. When the man who drives twenty miles to save one dollar is asked to rethink his behavior, watch out. We must be careful not to label greed the sin of the wealthy alone, for greed can take many forms. Greed is really a form of control, far more than a sin of acquisition. Greed is always accompanied by the need to control something or someone. The fiercest independent thinker will agree that holding onto "rugged individuality" provides a sense of control over life, however unreal that sense may ultimately be.

In this final spiritual crisis before death, the real issue is our desire to hold on to the people, places, and things that made up our lives, however modest or extravagant. We want to possess more than property or bank accounts. We want to possess people. We desire to hold on to those things that gave us pleasure. We are greedy in relationships, and we become territorial in our worldview.

In the woodcuts that teach medieval Christians about the temptation toward greed, we see Moriens surrounded by his wife, children, and friends.[2] A demon is pointing at his loved ones, as well as to his many possessions: his fine stable of horses, his well-stocked wine cellar, and his home. In one depiction the attempt to hold onto these things is made all the worse when Moriens sees a thief making off with wine from his cellar while he is too sick to do anything about it.

Today it may still be wine and horses, family members and dear friends that snare us in greed, and the fierce will to retain our life as we have known it. It might be the vacation home, the ski holidays, the getaway in Mexico, or the hard-won work of investments and labor. The Mercedes may replace the horse, the fine cuisine the personal wine cellar. But it is no different today than for our ancestors. We hang on for dear life. Fingernails clinging to the precipice, we will not let go. And greed really knows no class. We don't have to be rich to tenaciously want to possess other people. We don't have to play the stock market in order to want to keep our home when we really need to move into smaller quarters or even a hospice facility. We don't need to be CEOs of Fortune 500 companies to want to thwart our relatives from misusing our possessions or waiting for our inheritance. We are simply human, yet we are called to be increasingly Christlike.

This crisis is the crisis of letting go, of gradually relinquishing control of people, places, and things we have "owned" or held sway over. Careers, children, and personal possessions all fall into this category. They no longer can command our attention if we are to die well, and die at peace.

If we have followed the practice of living well, this crisis will be less powerful than if we have not. If we have learned to "let go" during our lifetime of health, we will meet this transition with greater grace and speed. If we have turned over our children to God's care, knowing they were but on loan to us, we will find peace more easily. If we have used our wealth to give back to our community, to the world in general, and to our families specifically, then this passage will be eased. If our affairs have been tended to before we get to the crisis—our wills made, our debts cleared, our lives in order—then we can rest in that knowledge, free from anxiety. If we have recognized any financial security we might have as the gift of God to be shared and passed on, we have done well. If we have taught others how to manage their affairs, if we have modeled generosity and kindness, then we will have little to fear from this crisis of greed. We will not be immune, but living well will prepare us to pass through this stage without terrible trauma.

If, however, we have not done these things, if we have not prayerfully attended to living well, then this final crisis will threaten to jeopardize our dying a peaceful death. The solution, as always, will be found in prayer and community. At this fifth stop in our stational liturgy, we seek the prayers that will heal our greed.

WOODCUT 5B

GENEROSITY

"'NON SIS AVARUS,' says the first good angel; 'Ne intendas amicis,' says the second, spreading a sheet before a man and a woman, presumably the son and daughter of Moriens, so that he may not be distressed at the sight of them. At the bed is a group of three women and two men, probably friends and relatives, together with a few sheep, which may represent his possessions. But closer to Moriens is the figure of Christ upon the Cross, with His Mother sorrowing beside Him, to remind the sick man of the extreme detachment from earthly things with which He approached His death. A fat little devil at the foot of the bed says, 'Quid faciam?'"[3] This is a tender picture of comfort and consolation. That which might further break his heart is veiled to grant him some protection in his final hour. It is Christ now and his mother, who looked upon her dying son and endured, who remain close to the soul of the dying Moriens.

Remedy: Generosity

"But strive first for the kingdom of God and his righteousness,
and all these things will be given to you as well."

MATTHEW 6:33

. . .

The antidote for greed is to practice generosity. That is why living well, living holy, is so important to the end of our lives. If we have not learned generosity before death appears on the horizon of our time on this earth, then we will struggle mightily. By seeking first the Kingdom of God in our lives, we turn our attention away from consumerism, mindless acquisitions, competitive and destructive behavior, the obsessive need to control, and we focus on the virtues that are known as the fruit of the presence of the Holy Spirit. The fruit of the Spirit, we are told by Saint Paul, is peace, love, joy, patience, kindness, generosity, faithfulness, gentleness, and self-control (Galatians 5:22-23). In order to reap these benefits, we must practice our faith, practice our discipleship, practice prayer, and practice the art of living well, which encompasses all these things. Living well *is* seeking first the Kingdom of God. It is having right priorities, and being as disciplined in spiritual matters as athletes, whether amateur or professional, are in their practice. We will all have different paces, different rates and periods of growth, but if we seek God first, then the fruit of the spirit will increase in our lives and accompany us at death.

In chapter three, I mentioned the veil of depression that clouded my own existence. I suggested that a veil has its place, but not a veil of blindness. Here in the final crisis, the crisis of greed, is where a veil becomes a

113

gentle, healing shroud. Again, turning to the woodcut depictions from the fifteenth century, we see the family and loved ones spreading a protective sheet between a man and a woman presumed to be the daughter and son of Moriens, who is dying, thus veiling him from the pain of seeing his loved ones and knowing he will soon depart from them.[4] It is to ease his suffering that he is veiled. Others gather at the foot of the bed, together with some sheep that may represent his possessions. But they are fading now from his vision. Drawing closer is Christ on the cross, the passion present until the end. Nearby is Mary, grieving by her son, reminding the dying man of the extreme detachment from earthly things with which Jesus faced death. This graphic display from the medieval imagination is actually very tender in its presentation of comfort and consolation. That which might further break the heart of Moriens should he see it has been veiled to grant him some protection in his final hour. It is now Christ and Mary, who remain close to the dying one . . . now and at the hour of his death, now and at the hour of our death.

To reiterate, the remedy to greed is generosity, the examination of our conscience as it relates to attachments, consumerism, and control, and the confession of our sins in sacramental form so that we may acknowledge our faults to ourselves, to God, and to another human being who stands in representation of God. It takes courage to confess, but the alternative is to be broken by guilt, greed, and the crises that will overtake us. If we practice generosity, if we practice letting go of control, if we seek first the Kingdom of God, then all will indeed be well. The holy anchoress and mystic, Julian of Norwich, was renowned for saying to those who sought her for spiritual direction: "All will be well, and all will be well."

Meditation

(FROM THE SEVEN LAST WORDS OF JESUS)

This meditation may be prayed as a multi-voice piece, within a liturgy, or it may simply be used for solo reading and meditation. For liturgical use, begin as chant, building in intensity. Follow with petition mode, presiding over the prayer of the gathered people, who join with Mary at the hour of Jesus' death. Resume chant-like oration wherever repetitions appear.

Mary's generous presence as a spiritual companion in holy dying is honored in this meditation. Once again, we turn to the Passion of Christ.

"Woman, Behold Your Son"

"Now and at the hour of our death, Amen."

"Now and at the hour of our death, Amen."

"Now and at the hour of our death—Amen!"

"*Now* . . . and at the hour of our death—Amen!"

Hail Mary! Oh blessed one, be near to us this moment of dread!

Your rejoicing, pliant spirit has walked the darkest valley of death.
Your recognition of the holy work of God was overshadowed
by the magnitude of suffering, the grand injustice
that tore the heart of heaven in two!
You wore the mantle of sorrow as mother of innocence,
courageous in your unspeakable pain.

115

Mary, Mother of Courage, pray for us.
Blessed among all people, cry out with us in protest!
Cry out for justice! Cry out in the name of Jesus!

Behold the work of hands that ply in trades of nails and thunder;
Behold the work of witnesses false, and envious deeds from below;
Behold the capital justice rushing out against the innocent One;
Behold the unstoppable outrage of our hearts!

Behold your Son, Mary . . .
Behold your Son . . .
Behold your Son!

He was once the child of the Temple Presentation;

Once the bold young boy who astounded the learned men;

Once the laughing friend of those who keep vigil with you;

Once Teacher,
Prophet,
Fisher of Disciples,
and the Way, the Truth, the Light.

Hail Mary, blessed with new life, now what has been wrought?

Dying before you, your Son hangs helpless;
You stand helpless;
But *stand*, Mary—Stand.

Weeping, you behold the price of love.
Weeping, you look upon the disciple John at your side,
given to you as son, his own face distorted with grief.
Your heart pierced and falling, spiraling, almost outside of yourself,
for what heart could contain this darkest hour of death?
This death of all deaths, this end of all hope,
this furious evil that claims the gift of love?

But you are blessed, Mary. You *are* blessed.
We have come to believe that you are blessed.
How can that be?
How can we believe that you are the chosen woman of God—
beloved and blessed beyond all measure?
Such terrifying blessing shakes the world!

• • •

Blessing—nailed to a cross,
Blessing—treated like a curse,
Blessing—falling to the ground in despair.
We bless you.
You never left, dear woman, as you beheld your son.

You never leave us, at the hour of our death.

Hail to you, dear Mary, who, faithful to the end,
beholds *what should not ever be*—beheld.

Hail to you, dear Mary, who teaches us to stay, to wait, to linger,
to receive—even to the receiving of the body of your Son.
Body and Blood, received in broken strength.

Continue to teach us the path of standing, staying, watching,
praying, and receiving.
Blessed are you who could see only darkness and sorrow,
yet who kept vigil, and kept faith.

Mary of Courage, Mary of the Sea of Sorrow, Mary of Mystery:

Stand near to us,

Now—and at the hour of our death, Amen.

May the peace of Christ be with you—in life, and in death.

R/. And also with you.

Prayer

Lord! Father of the Universe
And Father of all Creatures
Spirit and Matter
Today hear if she asks
The least of your children
Who loves you from the depths of her heart
Her happiness to live forever . . .
Before you like a child before his father
With neither pain nor suspicion
I start a New Year
In the beginning of the springtime.

What will I be? I am in your hands.
Respectful? . . . Yes.
Obedient? Hardly . . .
But may Your Will be done
And may a morsel of wisdom descend on my old age
So that my time will not be empty or vain
Give me love and Enlightenment
Sufficient to share with others who
Stumble and grope on the Way
The Way so narrow that leads to Eternity . . .

Amen.[5]

·VI·
Death

WOODCUT 6

THE DEATH OF MORIENS

"IN THIS SCENE, the only one in which Moriens is at the left, the soul, in the form of a small child, is passing from his body to one of the group of four angels behind the bed. A monk holds a candle in the hand of the dying man. On the left side stands a crucifix between two groups of saints, Our Lady, St. Mary Magdalene, and St. Peter (here distinguished by a sword) foremost in one group, St. John in the other. At the right of the bed six demons are departing in fury. 'Confusi sumus,' they say. 'Heu insania,' 'Furore consumor,' 'Animam amisimus,' 'Spes nobis nulla.'"[1]

Moriens has passed, safely, through the crises, borne up by the wondrously crowded map of the afterlife. He is never alone, but always in the company of the Church on earth and the communion of saints in the next world, including the saints most often associated with the borders between life and death. Scholar Eamon Duffy has noted that these included John the Baptist and Saint John the Evangelist, "who were both intercessors at the Judgement, or St. Peter," and especially the intercessions of Saint Michael the Archangel.[2]

Death

But we do not want you to be uninformed,
brothers and sisters, about those who have died,
so that you may not grieve as others do who have no hope.
For since we believe that Jesus died and rose again,
even so, through Jesus, God will bring with him those who have died.
Therefore encourage one another with these words.
1 THESSALONIANS 4:13–14, 18

. . .

Death comes. The five spiritual crises have passed. We have arrived at the final station of our pilgrimage through the *Ars Moriendi* tradition. We have learned that if we have lived well, we will have done the preparation necessary to meet these spiritual crises that arise on the final journey of our lives. The five crises of the medieval and Renaissance *Ars Moriendi* are as real today as they were at the time of the original handbooks.

In the twentieth century Elisabeth Kübler-Ross became famous for her research and theories on death and dying. Her view of the stages of death came to be regarded as a widely accepted road map of death and dying for our own time. The *Ars Moriendi* was an earlier map, and a specifically religious one. It was powerful enough in its wisdom to transcend the rupture of the Reformation and be carried on by both Roman Catholics and Protestants. Its wisdom remains with us today for the taking.

In the final woodcut, Moriens' soul, depicted as childlike, departs from a spiritual portal that emerges from the top of his head. He is carried off by a group of four angels. A monk stands at his bedside holding a candle symbolic of the baptismal candle and the light of Christ. On the left, a crucifix is situated between two groups of saints, Mary the Mother of Jesus, Mary Magdalene, and Saints Peter and John. On the other side of the bed, six demons flee in fury, vanquished by prayer and by Christ himself.[3]

Safe journey, Moriens. You were well cared for in your holy dying.

We can conclude that the wisdom of living well and dying well is clearly that we don't go it alone. Any retrieval of the practices and wisdom of this art means going beyond our comfort zones and being present for one another, so that death is not solitary. We in turn prepare ourselves for our own deaths.

We are not alone, but rather we are in the company of the Church on earth and the communion of saints of heaven. Saint Michael is present in the prayers and orations of the textual handbooks for the dying, second only to the Blessed Virgin Mary. Mary comforts, as Saint Michael defends our souls. Saint Michael is traditionally called upon in times of crisis, in spiritual battle, and in exorcistic prayers, whether minor or major.

In this sixth station of our pilgrimage, Moriens is resting in peace. It is clear, by practicing the exercises and remedies, by accompanying others so that we may learn our own way, and by seeking first the Kingdom of God during our lifetime, that peace may be ours as well. Live well, in order to die well. No one who neglects spiritual care and ethical living throughout their lifetime can expect to approach death with peace. The spiritual crises will be fierce for those unprepared. But for those who heed the wisdom of the elders and strive to live well, for those disciples of Christ, the crises will be less formidable, and the result will be peace.

This reflection on retrieving the art of living well and dying well has also focused on the Passion of Christ, as in earlier times. Christ suffered for us, suffered so that we might all endure, and is our salvation and peace in and through our own suffering. We are promised a share in the cross when we embrace Christianity. This is not an easy path. As M. Scott Peck said at the very beginning of his worldwide best-seller, *The Road Less Traveled*, "Life is difficult."

We have also been warned by Saint Paul that the cross is an offense to many: "For the message about the cross is foolishness to those who are perishing, but to us who are being saved it is the power of God" (1 Corinthians 1:18). Even among Christians we can experience deep resistance to the idea that the cross is necessary or that the Passion of Christ is a powerful spiritual meditation for transformation in times of suffering. At a time when a consumer mentality infects everything, including religion, people pick and choose what they will tolerate, and often the cross is the first thing to go from their belief system. Yet without the cross, there is no resurrection. Without the cross, there is no salvation. Without the cross, we cannot be transformed in Christ.

While I was writing this book, I engaged in conversation with a woman who considered herself to be a good Christian. She told me that she didn't like to see crucifixes in the hospital rooms of patients who were suffering from serious illness because it "would depress them." (Yet we have seen that this is the beloved practice of surrounding ourselves with sacramentals.) What they needed, if there were any cross at all, she declared, was one with a fully clothed, resurrected Jesus on it! *That* Jesus was acceptable. The dying Jesus, naked and suffering, was an offense to her. It made her uncomfortable, and she projected her own discomfort onto what she thought would be spiritually good for the sick and dying patients as well. This is not an unusual response. The cross is an ancient offense. But Jesus did not hide from the cross, and his disciples witnessed the agony of their beloved master, even if few of them stayed to watch and wait for death. Mary was there, and Mary Magdalene, and Mary the friend of Jesus, as well as John. Death was not hidden away in a hospital room. When Jesus was condemned to capital punishment it was not by lethal injection. It was by public crucifixion, though he was innocent. His death was particularly brutal. It was the way things were done in that culture and during that time in history in which God chose to send his Son. The mystery of suffering is a mystery that belongs to all of us.

Yet the cross holds a promise, and it is a paradox. Through it we are transformed. By his wounds we are healed. By his resurrection we have hope for our own. I hold the hope that those who make the decision about whether or not to display crucifixes in hospital rooms do not bow to thinking that finds the presence of the cross depressing or offensive. For the wisdom of our elders is being passed on to us, and that wisdom finds healing when our gaze fixes on the cross and the hope of the resurrection. Both/and, not either/or. We have not outgrown the cross, nor have we become so sophisticated that it no longer has any power over us. In fact it is the very power of Christ's passion that causes some to turn away.

The art of living well and dying well is rigorous, but it is worth it. As a nation we witnessed the very public death of the late Joseph Cardinal Bernardin of Chicago in 1996. Through it, we caught a glimpse of this holy art. This man of God lived well, and he died well.

Cardinal Bernardin was an especially well-loved bishop, but he had had his share of deep suffering. He had been falsely accused of sexual abuse by a former seminarian, an accusation that was later recanted, but not before it took a terrible toll on the cardinal. Some linked his diagnosis of cancer with the stress he underwent during this crisis in his life. Through the crisis of false accusations he lived well: he modeled forgiveness, truth, and poise. When, soon after, he faced his final crisis, that of cancer, he committed his final thoughts to writing in a memoir entitled *The Gift of Peace*. He died at peace with the world he lived in and in the peace of Christ. He gave us a great gift in sharing his final days so that we might pray with him and also so that we might learn the art of dying well. Cardinal Bernardin's memoir is very much in the tradition of the *Ars Moriendi*. It provides a contemporary model for the art of living well and dying well. We can be grateful to the late cardinal for sharing that gift of peace with us all. It is helpful if we look to those in our lives who have modeled holy living and holy dying. I pray that we all have such models.

And in the final journey of each who reads this, may perpetual light shine upon you and lead you into eternal peace.

Until then, rejoice, be glad, and live in gratitude for the gift of life itself.

Prayer

Dying Day

When your eyes are closing and your mouth opening,
  May God bring you comfort on that day.

When your senses are fading and your limbs growing cold,
  May God save your soul on that day.

Pray to Michael and to all the angels,
Pray to Mary and to all the saints,
  That God will pour out his mercy on that day.

Pray that the Virgin will reach out and embrace you,
That Michael will reach down and lift you up,
  On the day of your death.[4]

· VII ·
The Celtic
"Happy Death"

The Celtic "Happy Death"

. . .

Before we end this pilgrimage of faith, let me offer an extra stop along the way, a side trip to an even earlier practice of dying well. In the centuries after Saint Patrick revolutionized Ireland's world in the fifth century, there existed the tradition of the Celtic "happy death." This tradition provides a glimpse of the cross-cultural nature of the theology of living well and dying well, and will serve as an example from before the medieval and Renaissance period.

Among the Celts there existed the practice of having one's *anam cara*, or soul friend, assist the dying person through the recitation of death blessings. The soul friend, remember, is Irish or Celtic terminology for what we today call a spiritual director or spiritual mentor. This death blessing was known as "soul leading," or *fois anama*—soul peace. In the context of Celtic practice, this soul friend was a lifelong, intimate friend. The *anam cara* was a person who was there when one was healthy, and whose friendship only death could part. Indeed the friend would be present at the time of death. The death blessing would be intoned, or sung, and the family and friends surrounding the dying person would join in the blessing. The Holy Trinity would be invoked, as the Celtic imagination had always had a triune characteristic to it. The dying person would then be "signed," and the intonation would continue, often including references to crossing *abhuinn dubh a bhais*, the black river of death, or *cuan mor na duibhre*, the great ocean of darkness, or *beantaibh na bith–bhuantached*, the mountains of eternity. As the person was dying, the artful image held by the Celtic companions of a holy

131

death was that of the soul ascended "like a bright ball of light into the clouds."[1]

The following is an example of an actual Celtic Christian death blessing:

> God, omit not this woman from Thy covenant,
> And the many evils which she in the body committed,
> That she cannot this night enumerate.
>> The many evils that she in the body committed,
>> That she cannot this night enumerate.
>
> Be this soul on Thine own arm, O Christ,
> Thou King of the City of Heaven,
> And since Thine it was, O Christ, to buy the soul,
> At the time of the balancing of the beam,
> At the time of the bringing of judgment,
> Be it now on Thine own right hand,
>> Oh! on Thine own right hand.
>
> And be the holy Michael, king of angels,
> Coming to meet the soul,
> And leading it home
> To the heaven of the Son of God.
>> The Holy Michael, high king of angels,
>> Coming to meet the soul,
>> And leading it home
>> To the heaven of the Son of God.[2]

The compassionate and gentle behavior and ritual prayers surrounding the deathbed in Celtic practice is exactly what the later *Ars Moriendi* literature on the continent advocated when finding an *amicus aegroti*, the Latin

132

term for "a friend of the soul." In the Celtic example, we find an additional model of the art of dying well, with poetry and song, with ritual, and with the company of loved ones.

Finally, along the same lines, particular to the west of Ireland was the concept of *bas sona*, or happy death. It was implicit that to die well, to have this "happy death," one made a final confession, and then was anointed with the oil of the sacrament of extreme unction, while a death blessing was sung. Nothing consoled the living more than the knowledge that their beloved friend or family member had died well.[3]

The following prayer-poem comes from that "happy death" tradition:

Joyous Death

Death with oil,
Death with joy,
Death with light,
Death with gladness,
Death with penitence.

Death without pain,
Death without fear,
Death without death,
Death without horror,
Death without grieving.

May the seven angels of the Holy Spirit
and the two guardian angels
Shield me this night and every night
Till light and dawn shall come;
Shield me this night and every night
Till light and dawn shall come.[4]

Conclusion

W e have now completed our pilgrimage through the *Ars Moriendi* tradition, the art of holy dying. We have learned of the common crises that afflict the dying, and have gained insight into their spiritual remedies. We have learned that these same crises afflict the living during the crises that occur throughout one's life, in every loss, in every great change. At those times we have the opportunity to practice the *art*. Loss of Faith, Despair, Impatience, Spiritual Pride, and Greed are the names of the forces that snag our spirits and distort our souls as we face the prospect of loss and death. Inspirations that revitalize faith, hope, patience, humility, and generosity have shone in the darkness as the cure for the soul's ailments. We ask the ancient question, "What is it that ails you?" And we seek the healing balm found in Christ's own wounds. We touch the wounds of Christ in his passion in order that we may heal and be healed.

We have learned through this journey that the best medicine for the spiritual crises is to prepare ourselves by living well. Part of that preparation is the accompaniment of others as they face death. In so doing, we not only become generous disciples of Christ, but we prepare our own souls and spirits for our eventual death. We practice our faith. We exercise our spiritual life.

We saw that the proper medicine for crises was the intentional, sacramental life well lived, both at times of ease and at times of trouble. We learned that prayer is always and everywhere. We valued the human accompaniment within the community of faith; of songs sung in strong voices; of the sacrament of penance and reconciliation; of the Eucharist as nourishment, medicine, and life-giving sacrament; of the liturgies of healing and liturgies of lamentation; of the repetition of scriptural narrative; and of the stories of the holy women and men who have gone before us.

And we learned that to do this well, we cannot do it alone. One last time: We do not go it alone. This is a communal process. Dying alone is not the Christian way. It should not be what happens in the body of Christ.

And we have learned that in order to live well, we seek first the Kingdom of God. We cannot do that alone either. So this is a shared art, this way of the *Ars Vivendi* and the *Ars Moriendi*.

We have learned. We have meditated on the passion of Christ and on the art of dying well, and we have prayed.

Now it is time to return from our pilgrimage. We hope to be changed by pilgrimages. At least that is our intent at the point of embarkment, and that is certainly my hope for you as you read and pray with this book.

We expect transformation when we are in the presence of God, in sacrament, in liturgy, in prayer, and in our faith communities. For where two or more are gathered, there is Christ in the midst of them. So gather for living and gather for dying, that we may be one with Christ and with one another. Amen. Go in peace.

Endnotes

Introduction

1. Nancy Lee Beaty, *The Craft of Dying: The Literary Tradition of the* Ars Moriendi *in England* (New Haven and London: Yale University Press, 1970), 46.
2. Beaty, *The Craft of Dying*, 43-44.
3. U.S. National Conference of Catholic Bishops, *Pastoral Care of the Sick: Rites of Anointing and Viaticum.* Prepared by the International Commission on English in the Liturgy, a Joint Commission of Catholic Bishops' Conferences (New York: Catholic Book Publishing Co., 1983).
4. Ibid., 142.

I. The First Spiritual Crisis and Remedy

1. Mary Catherine O'Connor, *The Art of Dying Well: The Development of the* Ars Moriendi (New York: AMS Press, 1966), 116.
2. Ibid.

II. The Second Spiritual Crisis and Remedy

1. Mary Catherine O'Connor, *The Art of Dying Well: The Development of the* Ars Moriendi (New York: AMS Press, 1966), 116-117.
2. Ibid., 117.
3. Matthew 20:1-16.

4. Oliver Davies, and Fiona Bowie, eds., *Celtic Christian Spirituality: An Anthology of Medieval and Modern Sources* (New York: Continuum, 1995), 45. This prayer is attributed to Ciaran of Clonmacnois, an Irish monastery, but is likely from a later period. In the original litany, the first line was in Latin, with the rest of the prayer in the Irish language.

III. The Third Spiritual Crisis and Remedy

1. Mary Catherine O'Connor, *The Art of Dying Well: The Development of the* Ars Moriendi (New York: AMS Press, 1966), 117.
2. Ibid., 117–118.

IV. The Fourth Spiritual Crisis and Remedy

1. Mary Catherine O'Connor, *The Art of Dying Well: The Development of the* Ars Moriendi (New York: AMS Press, 1966), 118.
2. Figure 4A.
3. O'Connor, *Art of Dying*, 118.
4. Figure 4B.

V. The Fifth Spiritual Crisis and Remedy

1. Mary Catherine O'Connor, *The Art of Dying Well: The Development of the* Ars Moriendi (New York: AMS Press, 1966), 118.
2. Figure 5A.
3. O'Connor, *Art of Dying*, 118–119.
4. Figure 5B.
5. Oliver Davies, and Fiona Bowie, eds. *Celtic Christian Spirituality: An Anthology of Medieval and Modern Sources* (New York: Continuum, 1995), 231–232.

VI. Death

1. Mary Catherine O'Connor, *The Art of Dying Well: The Development of the* Ars Moriendi (New York: AMS Press, 1966), 119.

2. Eamon Duffy, *The Stripping of the Altars: Traditional Religion in England c. 1400-c. 1580* (New Haven and London: Yale University Press, 1992), 325.

3. Figure 6.

4. Robert Van de Weyer, ed., *Celtic Fire: The Passionate Religious Vision of Ancient Britain and Ireland* (New York: Doubleday, 1990), 157–158.

VII. The Celtic "Happy Death"

1. For more on this Celtic Christian practice of dying with the assistance of one's *anam cara*, see Oliver Davies and Fiona Bowie, eds., *Celtic Christian Spirituality: An Anthology of Medieval and Modern Sources* (New York: Continuum, 1995), 101–103.

2. Davies and Bowie, *Celtic Christian Spirituality*, 102–103.

3. Ibid., 141.

4. Ibid., 141–142.

Suggestions

for Further Study and Enrichment

Atkinson, David William, ed. 1992. *The English* Ars Moriendi: *Renaissance and Baroque Studies and Texts*. New York: Peter Lang.

Beaty, Nancy Lee. 1970. *The Crafte of Dying: The Literary Tradition of the* Ars Moriendi *in England*. New Haven and London: Yale University Press.

Davies, Oliver, and Fiona Bowie, eds. 1995. *Celtic Christian Spirituality: An Anthology of Medieval and Modern Sources*. New York: Continuum.

Duffy, Eamon. 1992. *The Stripping of the Altars: Traditional Religion in England c. 1400–c. 1580*. New Haven and London: Yale University Press.

Gula, Richard M. 1999. "Dying Well: A Challenge to Christian Compassion," *The Christian Century* 116 (May 5, 1999): 501.

Kubler-Ross, Elisabeth. 1969. *On Death and Dying*. New York: Macmillan Company.

O'Connor, Mary Catharine. 1966. *The Art of Dying Well: The Development of the* Ars Moriendi. New York: AMS Press Inc.

Spiro, Howard. M., McCrea Curnen, Mary G. and Palmer Wandel, Lee, eds. 1996. *Facing Death: Where Culture, Religion, and Medicine Meet.* New Haven and London: Yale University Press. Essays from the Yale Conference on the *Ars Moriendi.*

Taylor, Jeremy. 1650. *Holy Living and Holy Dying: Volume I: Holy Living.* P. G. Standwood, ed. Reprinted in critical edition, 1989. Oxford: Clarendon Press.

_____. 1651. *Holy Living and Holy Dying: Volume II: The Rule and Exercises of Holy Dying.* P. G. Stanwood, ed. Reprinted in critical edition, 1989. Oxford: Clarendon Press.

Suggested Music

Schroeder-Sheker, Therese. 1990. *Rosa Mystica* (German CD), Celestial Harmonies.